Ferry Services

of the

London, Brighton

&

South Coast Railway

by

S. Jordan

THE OAKWOOD PRESS

© Oakwood Press & S. Jordan, 1998.

British Library Cataloguing in Publication Data
A Record for this book is available from the British Library
ISBN 0 85361 521 7

Typeset by Oakwood Graphics.
Repro by Ford Graphics, Ringwood, Hants.
Printed by The Witney Press, Witney, Oxon.

LANDING AT DIEPPE. (PASSAGE CHOPPY)

A sorry group of passengers after a choppy crossing to Dieppe. *Author's Collection*

Front cover: SS *Dieppe* flies the LBSCR House Flag from her aft mast. *Author's Collection*

Rear cover: An official LBSCR/Ouest postcard poster extolling the virtues of the rapid service by day or night from Paris to London. *Author's Collection*

Title page: The ship's bell from the PS *Brighton* is on show in the National Railway Museum, York. Built in 1878 by Elder's of Glasgow, she, and her sister PS *Victoria* were the first steel-hulled vessels in the LBSCR fleet. *Author's Collection*

Published by
The Oakwood Press
P.O. Box 13, Usk, Mon., NP5 1YS.

Contents

The last vessel built for the LBSCR/LSWR Joint Co., the PS *Duchess of Norfolk*.
Author's Collection

3

BRIGHTON and FRENCH STATE RAILWAYS

Paris and the Continent

Via NEWHAVEN and DIEPPE.

TWO EXPRESS SERVICES DAILY.
24-Knot Turbine Steamers crossing Channel in 2¾ Hours.
CORRIDOR TRAINS.

France, Italy, Switzerland, South Germany, Austria, Spain, etc.

CYCLING AND MOTORING IN NORMANDY.—Every facility for the shipment of Motor Cars between Newhaven and Dieppe.

Excellent Roads and Scenery.

Full Particulars of Continental Traffic Manager,
Brighton Railway, Victoria Station, LONDON, S.W.
1913

Car ferry service, all vehicles travelled to France as deck cargo as can be seen in this 1913 advertisement.   *Author's Collection*

Introduction

From a small contractor's wharf at Shoreham Harbour the ferry services of the London, Brighton & South Coast Railway (LBSCR) grew to become the fourth largest railway-owned passenger ferry service in the United Kingdom. Following early legal setbacks the LBSCR quickly set up a thriving cross-channel service in partnership with the Western Railway of France, and later, with the London & South Western Railway, Portsmouth-Isle of Wight ferries.

In the 83 years the LBSCR was in existence it chartered, shared or owned over 125 different vessels, ranging in size from the largest cross-channel passenger ships to tiny pinnaces for passing messages in Newhaven Harbour. Some, the passenger vessels, were the height of luxury whilst a few, the non-revenue earning coal hulks, were rotten and barely afloat.

In its various guises the company vessels carried over seven million passengers and 1.5 million tons of cargo on the Newhaven-Dieppe route alone. During World War I 10 million allied troops and 11 million tons of war stores passed through the company's port at Newhaven.

This book attempts to set out, port by port, the fascinating history of this one railway company's successes (many) and failures (few) in the movement of passengers by sea.

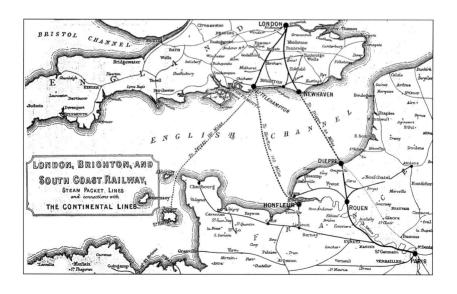

5

Only passengers with a strong stomach should eat on any but the calmest of crossings.

Author's Collection

Chapter One

Shoreham-Dieppe

The wharf at Kingston, in Shoreham Harbour at the mouth of the River Adur, was built in 1838 as a landing place for building materials for the use of Hayle and Wythes, the contractors for the Brighton to Shoreham section of the London and Brighton Railway (L&BR) 'West Coast Line'. On completion of the line in 1840 the wharf was taken over by the railway company. Kingston station opened on 12th May, 1840 and passengers were able to take passage to France on the General Steam Navigation Company's (GSNC) vessel PS *Magnate* from the wharf. Dieppe was the destination on Mondays, Wednesdays, Thursdays and Saturdays and Havre on Tuesdays and Fridays.

Further trade was created at the wharf when coke ovens were built in an area between the station building and Lower Road, which at this point ran alongside of the riverbank. The bulk of the coke used by the company's railway locomotives was produced at these ovens; the L&BR was able to produce its coke more cheaply, and to a higher grade and quality, than could be supplied by the local coal merchants.

In October 1843 the GSNC and the L&BR agreed to co-ordinate their timetables, beginning in April 1844. Two new vessels were purchased by the GSNC, the PS *Menai* and the PS *Fame*. Two weekly return trips were made between Shoreham and Dieppe, on Wednesdays and Saturdays. Passengers disembarking at Dieppe boarded a road coach to Rouen where they joined the Paris and Rouen Railway for the journey to Paris. So popular was this service that the L&BR set up a committee to look into the possibility of the railway company purchasing its own passenger vessels and keeping the profits to itself. The committee reported in November 1844, with the end result that ferry services did in fact start, not from Shoreham, but from Newhaven beginning in August 1845. A further blow to the wharf's business fell in 1849 when the London, Brighton and South Coast Railway, as the old L&BR had now become known, opened a new wharf at Deptford on the Thames in London. Coking plants were built in London and most of the coal was now landed there.

The loss of the passenger ferry and coal business did not effect the trade passing through Kingston too badly, though, as new firms had moved in locally and were making use of the wharf's facilities. A malt house was built adjacent to the coke ovens in 1844 and was leased by Valance and Catt who also ran what was to become known as the West Street Brewery. May and Thwaites opened a shipyard next to the wharf and here they built schooners, coal brigs and barques for local coal merchants. Finally Tooth and Co. erected a steam saw mill at the wharf to convert timber from North America and the Baltic into planks and building material.

LBSCR ferry boats did not stop coming to Shoreham Harbour completely though, as many of these vessels wintered at the wharf. Also ships requiring minor repairs or repainting which could not be carried out during a single low tide had to come here, as a dry dock facility was not available at Newhaven until 1882. The station at Kingston was one casualty of the withdrawal of the ferry services however and it was closed on 1st May, 1879 due to a lack of passengers. Company cargo vessels continued to use the wharf for the import of fruit and eggs from Normandy and also timber for Tooth's saw mill.

The track layout at Kingston is worthy of note, being unusual in so far as the wharf was at a lower level than the main line and was reached by means of an incline. Turntables were placed at either end of the slope giving access to the main line, the sidings at the coke ovens and the wharf proper. Wagons going up or down the incline were hauled by chains attached to a stationary engine at the top of the slope. Horses were used to shunt the wagons around the sidings. The use of small turntables and the size of the tunnel under Lower Road restricted the size of wagons able to use the wharf to a maximum wheelbase of 11 ft 9 in. and a height of 11 ft.

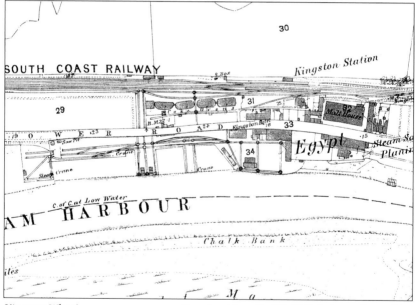

Kingston Wharf.   *Reproduced from the 25", 1860 Ordnance Survey Map*

Chapter Two

Newhaven-Dieppe

In the early 1840s Newhaven was a small fishing village situated on the mouth of the River Ouse, seven miles (west) of Brighton. On the face of it this would seem to be an unlikely place for a major cross-channel ferry port. In fact there were many reasons why it should have remained a sleepy harbour on the Sussex coast: it had no railways, country lanes were its highways, its waters were shallow and larger vessels could only navigate the top reaches of the harbour during the highest tides. So what happened to change the status of this humble haven from the lowest position to its high rank amongst the ports of southern England, second only to Dover on the south-eastern coast? As previously noted in the first chapter, the London & Brighton Railway set up a committee to report on the feasibility of creating a subsidiary company to run its own ferry services. In November 1844 the committee made its report to the Board. Not only were the financial aspects looked into but also several routes were inspected for possible use. The Shoreham/Brighton/Havre or Dieppe routes were ruled out because the extra hour required to load passengers at Brighton Chain Pier meant that the small underpowered craft used at this time would not be able to make the crossing in one high tide. Folkestone-Boulogne was also rejected for the same reason of tides. The committee's recommendation was that the most favourable route would be Newhaven-Dieppe, and that new vessels should be built that could, in normal weather conditions, make the crossing in five hours or less.

In March 1845, after a shareholders' meeting had approved the plan, the Newhaven Harbour Board was approached by the L&B and informed that it wished to make Newhaven a packet station. A request was made of the Harbour Board as to what facilities could be made available and what reductions in Harbour Dues could be expected. At the same time, to hedge its bets so to speak, a similar request was made of the Shoreham Harbour Board (SHB). The SHB sat on the request and, only after a long period, declined to improve on current facilities or charges. Newhaven however promised improvements in both details and was rewarded with the steamer service. In August 1845 the L&BR registered its subsidiary company as the Brighton and Continental Steam Packet Company (B&CSPC).

The main drawback to the establishment of a steamer service at Newhaven was the lack of a rail link, and so in January 1846 plans for a Newhaven branch line were included in a package of plans laid before Parliament under the long-winded title of 'An Act for making Railways from the Brighton, Lewes and Hastings Railway to Eastbourne, to Hailsham, and to Seaford and Newhaven. And certain deviations from the said Rly, all in the county of Sussex'. The Act received Royal Assent on 18th June, 1846. In the same month the Act for the formation of the B&CSPC was passed.

On 27th July, 1846 the L&BR merged with the London and Croydon Railway to become the London, Brighton and South Coast Railway. One of the new

An 1853 engraving of the London and Paris Hotel, Newhaven. Three Maples cross-channel
steamers are tied up to the Railway Wharf.   *Author's Collection*

The entrance to Newhaven Harbour as it was in the 1850s.   *Author's Collection*

company's first acts was to place an order with Thompsons of Rotherhithe for three wooden paddle steamers for the use of the B&SCSPC.

Towards the end of the year the Admiralty informed the LBSCR of its approval for a new wharf to be constructed at Newhaven. The General Steam Navigation Co. was by this time becoming increasingly upset with the idea of the railway company running ships in direct competition to itself, and so informed the LBSCR that from 30th November it would cease any joint sailings from Shoreham or Newhaven.

As the premier port for the Brighton Railway, it was decided that Newhaven should have a top-class hotel built on the quay for the use of passengers. The Board announced a competition to design just such a building with a prize of £100 for the winner. In May 1847 the winning design was announced, and much to the embarrassment of the Board it was discovered that the entry had been placed by four draughtsmen from the company's own Engineering Department, and so was ineligible for the prize. The Board were so pleased, however, that the four had done so well that they made them an ex-gratia payment of the £100 anyway.

In the spring of 1847 the B&CSPC commenced its steamer service to Dieppe with its three new vessels PS *Brighton,* PS *Dieppe* and PS *Newhaven.* Passengers still had to use a road coach between Newhaven and the nearest railway station, which was at Lewes, but in December the new double-track line between these two towns was opened. Intending passengers could now travel under steam power from London to Dieppe and from Rouen to Paris. Work had also commenced this year to forge the last link in the steam chain with the construction of the Dieppe and Rouen Railway. Some 2,400 navvies worked on the line and had almost completed their labours when civil unrest in France caused the mostly-British workforce to cease work whilst the riots blew themselves out. The line was completed by early July 1848 and opened to traffic on the 29th of that month. Ironically, now that the two capitals were linked by railways, fate played its hand and the central, seaborne, span was broken. The LBSCR's steamer subsidiary, the B&SCPC had been made to cease its packet services by force of law. The South Eastern Railway (SER), the Brighton's closest neighbour and rival, with its own steamer service from Dover to Calais to protect had become jealous of the Dieppe service's success. It had proved in the Chancery Courts that the LBSCR had no legal powers under its Act of Incorporation to run a steamship service, even through a subsidiary company. The SER's own ferry service was a joint venture with a private company, whereas the LBSCR was the major shareholder of the B&CSPC. This effectively put a stop to the ferry service for the summer season of 1848.

Left with no alternative, the LBSCR had to approach its old enemy the GSNC. On 7th August, 1848 the LBSCR asked the GSNC to take over the Newhaven-Dieppe service on the railway company's behalf. Knowing that the LBSCR had no other choice the GSNC pressed for an unnecessary deepening of the berth at Newhaven thus causing a 10-month break in the steamer service whilst the dredging took place. Finally in May 1849 the GSNC's vessel PS *Magician* resumed the steamer service.

Newhaven Harbour, *c.* 1855, the two paddle steamers would have been running under the authority of Mr Maples the LBSCR's shipping agent.

Author's Collection

The LBSCR was unhappy with the service provided and was very soon looking for a replacement. In July 1850 the company came to an agreement with Mr Henry Maples to provide vessels for a service between Newhaven and Jersey. The agreement shows that the service was to begin on 12th August and, weather permitting, two trips per week were to be made by the iron-hulled screw steamer SS *Ladybird*. A further clause in the agreement stated that the LBSCR would pay Maples £150 for the provision of a deck cabin to hold up to 14 passengers. As payment for his services Maples was to receive one-third of the receipts and also £365 per annum for acting as the railway's agent. This arrangement worked so well that by early 1851 Maples was approached to provide the vessels for the Newhaven-Dieppe route, payment to be on a similar basis as the previous agreement; Maples agreed.

In April 1851 the GSNC was informed once again that its services were no longer required as Mr Maples was to become the railway's main agent from 1st June, 1852. In November 1851 the LBSCR donated £10 and gifted 2 guineas annually for the provision of a lifeboat at Newhaven. Following an agreement between the LBSCR, the Paris Rouen Railway and Maples in February 1852, Maples was contracted to run the Newhaven-Dieppe steam packet service for a period of six years. He was to provide two return trips per week in the winter and six in the summer months, Tuesday to Sunday. A clause in the agreement gave Maples a loan using the SS *Ladybird* as collateral against any non-payment of the debt.

The vessels provided by Maples were not of the best quality, nor were they the newest ships available. In fact most of the fleet used were old Clyde steamers like PS *Rothesay Castle* an ancient steel-hulled paddle steamer built in 1837 by Tod and McGregor. It was purchased from William Denny and Bros of Dumbarton in 1851, and only lasted one summer season before being sold to Australia in November of that year. The PS *Ayreshire Lassie* was built in 1839 by Duncan's of Greenock, it was another of the vessels purchased by Maples from Denny in 1851 from stock on hand from the Burns Castle fleet of Clyde steamers. The *Lassie* also only lasted one summer season before being sold on, this time to a Liverpool company in early 1852. PS *Culloden* built in 1845 by Caird and Co. was purchased second-hand. Like the previous vessels it was only in service for one season, being sold to Melbourne at the end of 1852. Another ex-Clyde vessel was the PS *Duntroon Castle* the last of the Denny stock ships; built in 1842 by Anderson and Gilmore she was powered by two single cylinder engines producing 150 hp. PS *Paris* (I) was the only vessel purchased new for the service, it was built in Port Glasgow and this 237 tonne ship was powered by two 120 hp engines.

As can be seen most of these ships were so old and poorly maintained that most had to be withdrawn after only a few months service. To fill the gaps in the rosters as many as 21 vessels, *William Cory, Jas Dixon, Cockerill, Staffa, Aquilla, Vigilant, Marco, Samual Laing, Collier* and *Wave Queen* to name but a few, were chartered between 1851 and 1862. The crossing in some of the smaller vessels could be quite sickening (literally) as will be seen in this extract from a diary covering two weeks in September 1852:

Newhaven Harbour seen from the Fort in this *c.* 1855 engraving. *Author's Collection*

Newhaven Harbour viewed from the east, *c.* 1855, in the foreground are the railway sidings with the harbour and town beyond. *Author's Collection*

Monday 13th. Morn at the British Museum, afternoon at Newhaven. Put up at the Railway Hotel (London & Paris Hotel), where Louis-Philippe (Emperor of France) stayed when he fled from France in 1848. We had procured our passports.

Tuesday 14th. 8 am. Leave by steamer for Dieppe; had a fine passage across. Arrive at 1, disembark at the Custom House where we were detained till too late for the next train.

Wednesday 15th. Start at 3 (from Rouen) for Paris, express train. Get there at 5.

Tuesday 18th. Very wet morning; railway station at 8. Plenty of confusion - dripping passengers looking for their packages and lost friends. After getting our luggage ticketed, we ensconced ourselves in the corner of a 1st class carriage. Two other passengers came in. We whisked away towards Rouen, where we arrived at 11. The weather cleared up and we had a pleasant run to Dieppe, which we reached at 1 pm. Found the *Wave Queen* a long narrow, iron steamer we had noticed on our first crossing, ready to start. After much turning ahead, backing, and bumping against the piers, we got out of harbour about 2, meeting *Paris* steamer going in. The weather looked squally and it soon commenced to blow in heavy squalls, with lightning and hailstorms. We had between 50 and 60 passengers, most of whom were sick enough from the ugly motion of this wavy craft. All of them in the Tee Saloon (a glass house on the deck, which I thought the sea would smash in). It soon became very close and smelly, as the doors and windows had to be kept closed. The weather continued to get worse, heavy squalls from SE and SW. We were both sick, I worse than Lizzie. 7 pm. Beachy Head light in sight. Blowing a gale. The tide not being sufficiently high to enter Newhaven piers, we stood out to sea again; the ship rolling her paddles under. The vessel, from her great length and small power, would not come round to the sea. A shocking scene in the overcrowded saloon, passengers all sick, ladies fainting, screaming, praying, the wind howling, and the sea striking the glass sides of the saloon with great violence, I thought it would smash in. Everything rolling about, crockeryware and glass smashing. To add to the confusion we had a raving lunatic on board who was screeching the most outrageous nonsense, the old Steward and Stewardess trying to pacify him, and endeavouring to quiet the frightened ladies, although they did not seem very comfortable themselves. At 9.30 stood in again towards the shore, and I could see the white line of breakers. We tried to run in between the piers, but in the heavy sea the vessel would not steer and we drifted broadside on to the breakers and took the ground to the eastward of the harbour. Then she bumped heavily, and the sea made a clear breach over us. I managed to scramble out to see the situation. I saw the crew getting over the bow and getting on shore by a rope, so I scrambled back to the cabin and got Lizzie to scramble out after me, dragging herself along by the ropes, for no one could stand. The vessel twisted about so, I thought she would have broken in half. We got forward to the bows. There was no one there, all the crew had gone. I saw a stout hawser hanging from the starboard bow and a lot of coastguardsmen below, so I got Lizzie to scramble over the bulwark and slide down the hawser to the coastguardsmen, who were ready to receive her, but just then a wave took her up to the neck, but a sturdy coastguardsman caught hold of her and dragged her up the beach. I followed and we got into the boat house, but of course we were soaked to the skin. The rest of the passengers soon followed. We then had to scramble along the embankment, which was so slippery we were nearly blown into the canal as the storm continued. After crossing the harbour in a small boat, we got to the hotel in a pretty plight, about midnight, and as our luggage was in the steamer, we borrowed clothes from the chambermaid and the waiter, regardless of fit, they were both small people. However, we soon turned into a comfortable bed. Where the other passengers were stowed, I do not know.

Wednesday 29th. The storm was over; all our luggage, which was left to the mercy of the wind and waves last night, was got out of the vessel this morning, which was left

PARIS, viâ Newhaven and Dieppe (special daily
service with new and fast STEAMERS).

Last Train from London-bridge.	Steamer leaves Newhaven.
June 28, at 8 a.m.	June 28, at 11 a.m.
June 29, at 10 a.m.	June 29, at noon.
June 30, at 10 a.m.	June 30, at 1 p.m.

Fares—London to Paris, 24s. and 17s. ; cabin and second class, 20s.
To Dieppe, 18s. and 14s. Apply at the Brighton and South Coast
Railway Stations ; or to Henry P. Maples, 5, Arthur-street east.

RAIL and STEAM.—London to Caen.—The
favourite screw steamer COLLIER is intended to sail from
Newhaven, on Tuesday, the 29th of June, at 7h. 30 p.m., for CAEN
direct, in connexion with the Brighton and South Coast Railway.
Fares—1st class, 21s. ; 2d class and best cabin, 17s. ; 3d class, 10s. 6d.
Apply to Henry P. Maples, 5, Arthur-street east.

Two advertisements by Maples from the *Times* of 1st June, 1852 showing timetables for the Newhaven vessels. *Author's Collection*

This very early view of Newhaven Harbour, c. 1855, shows two of the vessels used by Mr Maples during his nine years as the LBSCR's shipping agent at Newhaven. *Author's Collection*

high and dry on the beach as the tide receded. We lost nothing thanks to the coastguardsmen, for whom we got up subscription amongst the passengers. They deserved it. We left for London by the 1 pm train and got to town between 3 and 4.

As can be seen from the above passage early crossings could be more eventful than the holiday itself!

In 1854 the Crimean War began and PS *Paris* and PS *Rouen* were commandeered to run the Russian blockade around the war zone. PS *Rouen* was captured on her second run but was released in 1855 following the cessation of hostilities. Notwithstanding the problems of PS *Wave Queen* and also the PS *Rouen* which hit a pier whilst entering Dieppe harbour in September 1853, and also had to back out of Le Treport after having mistaken it for Dieppe in bad weather, the LBSCR and the Paris Rouen Railway were very happy with the service provided by Mr Maples. So much so that in July 1855 the agreement of 1852 was extended from six to ten years. This was on the condition that Maples placed five vessels on the route, and provide a daily service, except Sundays all-year round. One vessel was to act as a replacement for any regular ships needing repairs and the others were to make one crossing every other day, spending one full day in port to load and unload cargo, the vessels being capable of carrying at least 20 tons.

Also in 1855 Thomas Cook and Sons, the travel agents, began to use Newhaven-Dieppe for its excursions to the Continent. Cook was granted preferential fares on the route provided he used Newhaven exclusively. Maples ordered three new vessels to fulfil the conditions of his extension as agent for the shipping line. PS *Dieppe* was built in London, and sister ships PS *Lyons* (I) and PS *Orleans*, iron-hulled boats powered by twin-cylindered engines producing 160 hp were built by J. Scott Russell.

In 1856 the LBSCR and Maples had a new partner when the Dieppe Rouen Railway, the Paris Rouen Railway and others merged to become the Chemin der fer de L'Ouest, or Western Railways of France. In 1857 Maples purchased the PS *Brighton* (II). She was iron-hulled, 193.5 feet long and 20.9 feet wide and was powered by two twin-cylindered engines producing 140 hp at a working pressure of 20 lb. Money problems caused Maples to sell this boat after only a few months. By early 1858 Maples was finding it increasingly difficult to keep his financial head above water. The cross-channel ferry service was only one string to his bow, but it was the only one making a profit. Only by mortgaging four more of his own boats to the LBSCR was he able to keep his other businesses afloat. Finally by late 1858 he was unable to meet the repayments on the mortgages, and he withdrew completely from the management of the shipping service in early 1859. On 22nd June, 1859 the LBSCR and the Ouest set up a joint agent to run the shipping service on their behalf. The agent, M. Bosson, was to be paid a salary of £480 per annum with an extra £120 for travelling expenses. Offices were set up in Paris, London, Newhaven and Dieppe. Mr Bosson was employed to run the service with limited powers, he could only act under the supervision of the two holding companies and was unable to 'hire and fire' captains, engineers or superintendents of the fleet without the permission of his supervisors. Receipts from ticket sales were to be split thus, Maples' boat account 44 per cent, Ouest 37 per cent, and the LBSCR 19 per cent. The portion for the Maples' boat account was to repay the mortgages on the five boats that Maples had borrowed money against. Early in 1862 the original hand-operated cranes at Newhaven were replaced with more efficient steam cranes capable of lifting much heavier loads.

In October 1862 'Four Sussex Gentlemen' undertook a weekend's 'adventure' in France; their report in the *West Sussex Gazette* tells us that the crossing on the PS *Orleans* was done in 'smooth and beautiful' conditions, and after a fine beefsteak in the captain's cabin they landed in Dieppe 'as fresh as larks' after a five hour crossing. The report continues with the following description of what happened after they left the boat for their first visit to France.

> Dieppe is a somewhat old and irregular sort of town, and on landing one sees some of the roughest omnibuses and horses, and the queerest looking drivers and conductors, possible. They all look as if the regular drivers and horses and harness had gone out for the day to some fete, and that an odd lot had been collected together to do duty for the time.
>
> The traveller, however, is not allowed to pass on his way quietly, for there are at different points cocked-hatted and red-trousered looking men, dressed like English generals, but known as Gendarmes, who point out the way to go. Entering a low shed-like place, called the Custom House, you pass a barrier as if you were about to take a railway ticket; but behind this barrier you see some stern-looking official, with peculiar caps and costume, and you feel almost as if you were to be dealt with by the Inquisition. The chairman of the Inquisition then looking at the well matured form of Robinson, said 'Englise?' and, receiving the unmistakable reply, the four voyagers passed on, with a very polite bow.

Once clear of the Customs formalities our four travellers met the next obstacle:

> The next thing is to unlock your portmanteau, and the custom house officer merely examines casually the character of your luggage and on you go. Pardon! there is one more stoppage as you leave the building. An old man sits at a table with some cash before him, as if he were ready to play some game of chance, and as we approach him he shouted 'Treepence!' [*sic*] as quickly as if someone had pulled a string to make the sound. We each paid our three pence, and toddled away.

After a happy weekend in Normandy the four leave Rouen by the 7.15 Monday morning train for Dieppe and by 10 o'clock they are back on board the PS *Orleans* for the journey home.

> The Steward gave us a good breakfast to start with, I put a cushion behind my back, and prepared for a read. As the steamer cleared the harbour, however, I became sensible of a peculiar dizziness, and I quickly made for the deck. 'It will be a rough'en' one and all exclaimed. The wind pointed at the nose of the steamer, and ere we had got a mile out, the sea lashed over the vessel furiously. Passengers began to wrap themselves up, and the obliging little egg-shaped steward hopped about from one to the other cheerfully making them up comfortable, lending coats and caps and shawls from his very extensive wardrobe.

After a sickening six-hour crossing the PS *Orleans* battled into Newhaven and the four gentlemen's adventure was over.

It was now time for the ferry service run by the LBSCR and the Ouest to be placed on a firm legal basis, determined not to be in a position whereby competitors could compel the closing of the service, as in 1847. Parliamentary powers were applied for under a portion of the LBSCR (Stations and Co.) Act 1862. Part of this Act states:

> . . . that it is expedient that the company should be authorised to build, charter, hire, maintain and work steamboats and other vessels in communication with the railways of the company, for the conveyance of traffic between the ports of Newhaven and Dieppe.

The Act received Royal Assent as 25 & 26 Vict. cap. 67 of 1862. Although the LBSCR now had full legal powers to run its own ferry services, it did not implement them fully until 1863 when the Maples' debt was cleared and his vessels were sold to other buyers or acquired by the joint company. Ex-Maples' craft PS *Lyons* (I) and PS *Orleans* (I) were purchased for £8,000 each, and three new vessels were purchased from Wigram, Richardson & Co. of Newcastle for £4,160 each. These were the sister ships SS *Rouen* (I) and SS *Sussex* (I) both cargo vessels, and the PS *Normandy* (I). The PS *Alexandra*, built by Caird and Co. of Greenock, was purchased for £15,900 and the last of the new vessels for the service was the PS *Marseilles* powered by a twin cylinder 190/200 hp engine which produced a top speed of 13 knots, which was ordered in 1864 from Lungley's for £17,000.

An article in the *West Sussex Gazette* of 7th May, 1863 gives us a first-hand view of one of the new vessels. Under the headline of 'A smart new steamer for the channel service', the report continues:

> The passage from Newhaven to Dieppe is likely to be shortened about one-third the time by the use of a very splendid new steamer which has just been built expressly for this service. The splendid new paddle steamer *Alexandra* built by Messrs Caird and Co., Greenock . . . arrived here on Friday last. The *Alexandra* is 535 tons o.m., 200 ft long, 23½ feet broad, and her depth of hold is 11 ft. She has a pair of oscillating engines of 200 horse power nominal, 52 inch cylinders, 4 ft 9 in. stroke, and a double set of large tubular boilers, one before and one abaft the engine. The paddle floats are feathered. She is measured to carry 243 passengers in the fore deck and 243 passengers in the after deck - in all 486 deck passengers. The *Alexandra* has been finished in a style of magnificence rarely, if ever, equalled. Her after saloon is 39 ft in length and seven feet in height, and admirably lighted. The ceiling is painted flatted white; mouldings, ornaments, etc., are done up in gold, crimson Utrecht velvet cushions, etc. Fore and aft are placed very large mirrors, in frames elaborately carved and gilt. The ladies' cabin is 18 ft long and 23 ft broad, and finished in an equal if not superior style.

After further descriptions of the interior the reporter turns his gaze on to the exterior of the vessel.

> She is flush- decked, has two funnels, and is rigged with two pole mast, and the general disposal and appearance of the main deck is beautiful, being fitted up with skylights, companions, accommodation for the Captain and all the Officers, four water closets, and other houses and conveniences, equal in style to any first class gentleman's yacht. At

Entrance to Newhaven Harbour, 1871.   *Author's Collection*

A fanciful engraving of Newhaven Harbour from the 1874 LBSCR illustrated guide.
                                                                       Author's Collection

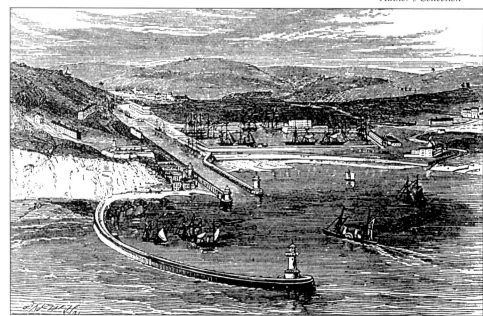

her trial trip she ran the distance, 15¾ knots in 54 minutes, and but for the thickness of the weather preventing the course being taken in a direct line, the distance could easily have been run in three minutes less.

Capital for the purchases were provided by the two companies to the ratio of LBSCR 19/56 and Ouest 37/56. Division of receipts was LBSCR 19 per cent, Ouest 37 per cent and the Joint Steamboat Account 44 per cent. The agreement binding the two companies together was signed in Paris on 1st September, 1864 to apply retrospectively from 1st July, 1863.

Following extensive earthworks at Newhaven the so called 'New Cut' was opened on the River Ouse in 1864. This straightened out a bow in the river to the north of the Railway Wharf and in the process cut off the only river crossing in the Newhaven area, an old wooden drawbridge erected in 1794. To replace the drawbridge an iron swing bridge was built at the southern end of the cut.

A new vessel was added to the fleet in 1865, PS *Bordeaux* (I) was the sister ship of the PS *Marseilles* and was built by Lungley of London.

Only 27 months after the inauguration of the joint service it had its first serious accident. At 2.30 am on 7th September PS *Alexandra* left Newhaven for Dieppe with 27 passengers on board. Whilst in the English Channel the vessel ran into a thick sea fog; not having modern navigation aids the Captain slowed the ship as it approached the French coast and sent one of the ship's lifeboats ahead to feel the way. Unfortunately this action was carried out too late to save the ship and she ran aground on the Cap d'Ailly. The passengers and crew manned the life boats and all were carried safely to the nearest French port. The PS *Alexandra* although badly holed, was saved and towed away for repairs at Le Havre. Fortunately she was back in service for May 1867, as Thomas Cook, acting as the LBSCR's managing agent for the 1867 Paris Exhibition, had organised over 20,000 visitors all needing berths on the Newhaven-Dieppe route.

The post of General Agent, held by Mr Bosson, was abolished in 1869 and the agencies were run by the Joint Company from its own railway premises. The 15th July, 1870 saw the outbreak of the Franco-Prussian War, after a series of disastrous military reverses at the battles of Woerth, Gravelotte and Sedan the French capital, Paris, was under siege by German troops. Railway services from Dieppe to Paris were suspended, but the ferry continued to make its nightly run until 9th December when German soldiers entered Dieppe. Fighting ceased on 28th January, 1871 with the capitulation of Paris and the ferry service resumed three days later on the 31st. Further disruption to the Dieppe-Paris rail route occurred during the period of the Commune, 28th May to 28th June, when large parts of Paris were taken over by revolutionaries. A peace treaty between the French and Germans was signed at Frankfurt-am-Main on 10th May, and, following the crushing of the Paris Commune, German troops began to leave France. By 3rd June German troops were out of Dieppe and the full ferry and railway service resumed operation.

Following the end of the war passenger numbers continued to rise steadily, no doubt helped by the alliance with Messrs Thomas Cook & Son, and so in 1873 year-round 'Night Service' sailings in each direction were established. This regular service was supplemented with extra daily sailings during the

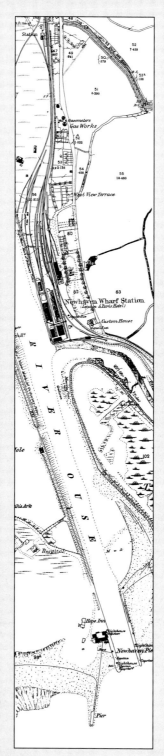

Newhaven Wharf and pier.
*Reproduced from the 25", 1872
Ordnance Survey Map*

summer season. Another facility for passengers was added in 1874 when the railway was extended from the Gare de Ville, Dieppe, through the streets to Quai Henry Quatre thus enabling passengers to join the Paris train directly after passing through the Customs House. The upsurge in passengers from 37,000 in 1871 to 61,000 in 1875 stretched the available resources to such an extent that three new vessels were ordered.

The SS *Newhaven* (II) and SS *Dieppe* (III) were cargo ships and were the first contribution to the fleet by the French partners. Built at Le Havre by Forges et Chantiers de la Mediteranee they were sister ships and identical in all but minor details of machinery. The Board of Trade and Lloyds were both unhappy with these ships as launched and considerable structural work had to be carried out before the vessels could be registered. The third ship was the SS *Paris* (II), a passenger vessel. She was designed by William Stroudley, the chief mechanical engineer of the LBSCR. She was a masterpiece of design and elegance, built in Glasgow by John Elder, her twin cylinder compound engines producing 200 hp. The original specification stated that the vessel should have not less than 36 first class cabins, 16 first class ladies' cabins and space for 207 first class passengers, also not less than 22 second class cabins, 16 second class ladies' cabins and space for 218 second class passengers. It further required that the cushions in the first class saloon should be covered in best crimson Utrecht velvet. She entered service in 1875.

The following year the LBSCR obtained Parliamentary permission to purchase all property belonging to the Newhaven Harbour Commission thereby taking over complete responsibility for running the port. The company, however, decided not to make full use of its powers and in 1878 formed the Newhaven Harbour Company (NHC) retaining full authority to manage it in perpetuity. Once the NHC had taken over management of the port from the Commission it began a full programme of improvements to the harbour. Included in the list of works to be carried out was the construction of a new quay to the south of Railway Wharf, to be known as East Quay, and the building of a massive breakwater, 2,800 feet long, at the mouth of the river. To carry out dredging operations, needed to deepen the berths to allow for non-tidal sailings, the LBSCR purchased the PS *Neptune*, a dredger built in 1877 by W. Simmons & Co.

New vessels purchased by the joint service to assist in carrying the expected rush of visitors to the great Paris Exhibition of 1878 were the sister ships PS *Brighton* (I) and PS *Victoria*. Built by John Elder of Glasgow they were the first steel-hulled vessels in the fleet and were fitted with steam steering also an innovation at Newhaven. The machinery was designed by William Stroudley, and the fixed cylinder engines turned 17 ft diameter paddle wheels which drove the ships along at a top speed of 16 knots. Shortly after joining the fleet PS *Brighton* (I) made the cross-channel run in only three hours and 54 minutes. PS *Orleans* now 22 years old, was sold out of service. To assist PS *Neptune* in its dredging tasks the SS *Trident*, a hopper vessel, was purchased in 1879. The following year another non-revenue earning vessel joined the fleet, she was the tug SS *Pinafore*. In 1881 the last wooden-hulled ferry to join the service was acquired, she was the PS *North Kent*, an old London Steam Boat Co. ship built in 1863.

An early photograph of the PS *Victoria* in her berth at Newhaven. Launched in 1878 its engines, designed by the LBSCR's CME William Stroudley, propelled the vessel at a top speed of 16 knots.
Author's Collection

PS *Bordeaux* tied up alongside the London and Paris Hotel in an 1886 advertisement for the hotel.
Author's Collection

THE LONDON AND PARIS HOTEL,

NEWHAVEN HARBOUR.

THIS HOTEL,
ADJOINS THE
NEWHAVEN HARBOUR
STATION PLATFORM
AND THE
CONTINENTAL
STEAMBOAT QUAY.

☞ The Tariff has been fixed at a most moderate Scale.

EVERY
ACCOMMODATION
AND
COMFORT
PROVIDED FOR
TRAVELLERS
EN ROUTE
TO AND FROM THE
CONTINENT.

WINES IMPORTED DIRECT.

Communications addressed to the undersigned will receive prompt attention.

J. BRADFORD, Proprietor.

The year 1882 saw the introduction of two new boats to the joint fleet, these were the sister ships PS *Brittany*(I), and the PS *Normandy* (II). They were both fitted with a new technical advance, self-feathering paddles. Designed once again by the mechanical genius William Stroudley, each wheel had nine steel floats attached, thus enabling each float to take a bigger bite on the down thrust and then slip easily out of the water on the up stroke. This increased speed without the necessity of increasing the engine's power. To free the name for the new vessel the old *Normandy* was renamed PS *Rouen* (II).

Work was now complete on the marine workshops at Newhaven and with the construction of giant sheerlegs, of 80 tons capacity and 118 feet high, and with the removal of the Gridiron (a large metal framework on which vessels could be rested for repair at low tide) from the ramp berth to a location nearer the workshops, they were opened for use. This year also saw the first publication of the joint companies' Continental Timetable giving details of its 'Daily Express Tidal Service', made possible by the improvements to the docks at Newhaven. A short-lived sideline for the LBSCR was a cargo service to the French port of Honfleur, but this was to last only one summer season.

The old girl PS *Alexandra*, having given good service from Maples' time, was sold in 1883. An even older ship, the SS *Lyons* (I), was sold in 1885. During its long service of 31 years it had been converted from paddles to screw and had ended its days with the company as a cargo ship. Two new cargo vessels joined the fleet in this year, the sister ships PS *Lyons* (II) and PS *Italy*, built by Elder's of Glasgow. In 1886 the new East Quay, begun in 1878, was opened. A new railway station had been constructed on the quayside and from now on all passenger sailings left from there instead of the old Railway Wharf. Around this time the vessel PS *North Kent* was disposed of, and the following year the old PS *Sussex* (I) was sold.

During the Easter holidays of 1887, on 13th April, PS *Victoria* was involved in a tragic accident off the Pointe d'Ailly near Dieppe. Making the crossing in a thick fog the Captain misjudged his position and ran aground. Whilst a full lifeboat was being lowered a woman's scarf became entangled in the pulley and upset the boat: 19 people were drowned. PS *Victoria* was a total loss, being broken up by the incoming tide.

In 1887 a decision was taken to man all passenger vessels with English crews and the cargo ships with French, resulting in the newest cargo boats being renamed in the French spelling, *Italie* and *Lyon*. On 20th November a fire badly damaged the new East Quay railway station.

Changes to the shipping list for 1888 included the sale of the old PS *Paris* (II) and the introduction of two new vessels, the PS *Paris* (III) and PS *Rouen* (III). Built by Fairfield and Co. of Glasgow, the successors to Elder's, these two ships were identical in all details and were ordered for the expected boost to trade from the Paris Exhibition. Licensed to carry 706 passengers, they were 250 feet long with two upright funnels and twin masts and were the last paddle steamers to be built for the Newhaven-Dieppe route.

On 11th September PS *Paris* broke the record for the channel crossing, making the trip in three hours and 25 minutes; only one day later PS *Rouen* beat that time by five minutes. Fitted with compound diagonal engines and boilers with forced draught, their top speed was 19¼ knots.

Pictured on the mud flats in Newhaven Harbour the PS *Normandy*, 1882, featured self-feathering paddles which improved the movement of the float through the water and produced higher speed without having to increase engine power.
B. Cakebread

PS *Paris*, launched in 1888, was brought into the fleet to help cope with the expected rush of passengers travelling to the Paris Exhibition. 250 ft long, she was licensed to carry 706 passengers.
B. Cakebread

FRIDAY TO TUESDAY AT DIEPPE

CHEAP RETURN TICKETS

ARE ISSUED

EVERY FRIDAY AND SATURDAY,

AVAILABLE TO RETURN UP TO THE FOLLOWING TUESDAY,

From London Bridge, Victoria, Kensington, Clapham Junction, East Croydon, Brighton, Tunbridge Wells, Uckfield, Lewes, Newhaven, Seaford, Eastbourne, St. Leonards, Hastings, Worthing, Littlehampton, Bognor, Chichester, and Portsmouth.

First Class, 26s.; Second Class, 19s.

These Tickets are available to and from Newhaven by any Train.

CHEAP RETURN TICKETS TO HONFLEUR.

SPECIAL CHEAP RETURN TICKETS, available for One Week, are issued from Brighton, Worthing, Littlehampton, Chichester, Havant, Portsmouth, and Newhaven Harbour to Honfleur.
Fares: First Class, 20s.; Second Class, 15s.; Third Class, 10s.

EXPRESS GOODS AND PARCELS SERVICE,

LONDON AND PARIS.

In order to meet the requirements of this important Traffic, the

LONDON BRIGHTON & SOUTH COAST & WESTERN OF FRANCE RAILWAY COMPANIES

Have made arrangements for the conveyance of

PARCELS, MERCHANDISE, BULLION, & ARTICLES OF VALUE,

BY

Special Passenger Trains and Boats between London and Paris,

Via NEWHAVEN, DIEPPE, and ROUEN,

AT CONSIDERABLY REDUCED THROUGH RATES.

The several improvements recently made in this Service ensure to the Public the greatest possible facilities, and the quickest attainable despatch in the transit of their Goods.

Custom-house Officers are in attendance at the Paris (St. Lazare) Station to clear all Goods forwarded for home consumption or for further transit.

The Trains run alongside the Steamers, both at Newhaven and Dieppe, and the Goods are loaded and unloaded direct from and to the trucks, thus avoiding cartage and consequent delays and damage to the Goods.

Parcels and Goods received up to 7.30 p.m. at the Paris or London Bridge Passenger Stations will be forwarded the same night.

The Rates include all charges except Customs Duty, French Government Stamps, and Statistical Tax.

CONTINENTAL PARCELS RATES to Dieppe, Rouen, Paris, Honfleur and Caen, exclusive of French Tax of 1d. per package, and 4d. per consignment. The Rates to and from London apply to any Station on the London Brighton and South Coast Railway other than Newhaven.

London to Paris Not including Collection or Delivery	Newhaven to Paris and vice versa. Not including Collection or Delivery.	London to Rouen and vice versa. Not including Collection or Delivery.	London to Dieppe and vice versa. Not including Collection or Delivery.	Newhaven to Dieppe and vice versa. Not including Collection or Delivery.	London to Honfleur and vice versa. Not including Collection or Delivery.	London to Caen and vice versa. Not including Collection or Delivery.
Not exceeding s. d	Not Exceeding s. d.	Not exceeding s. d.	Not exceeding s. d.	Not exceeding s. d.	Not exceeding s. d.	Not exceeding d.
2 lbs. 1 1	2 lbs. 1 1	2 lbs. 1 1	2 lbs 1 0	2 lbs. 0 8	7 lbs. 1 3	7 lbs. 3
11 ,, ... 1 8	11 ,, ... 1 5	11 ,, ... 1 4	11 ,, ... 1 3	11 ,, ... 1 0	14 ,, ... 1 9	14 ,, ... 2 11
22 ,, ... 2 6	23 ,, ... 2 6	22 ,, ... 2 5	22 ,, ... 2 0	22 ,, ... 1 7	28 ,, ... 2 3	28 ,, ... 3 9
33 ,, ... 3 3	33 ,, ... 3 3	33 ,, ... 3 3	33 ,, ... 3 0	33 ,, ... 2 4	56 ,, ... 2 9	56 ,, ... 4 8
44 ,, ... 4 0	44 ,, ... 4 0	44 ,, ... 3 10	44 ,, ... 3 6	44 ,, ... 2 8	84 ,, ... 3 3	84 ,, ... 5 9
66 ,, ... 4 6	66 ,, ... 4 6	66 ,, ... 4 6	66 ,, ... 4 0	66 ,, ... 3 6	112 ,, ... 4 3	11 ,, ... ·1
88 ,, ... 4 10	88 ,, ... 4 10	88 ,, ... 4 10	88 ,, ... 4 5	88 ,, ... 4 0		
110 ,, ... 5 3	110 ,, ... 5 3	110 ,, ... 4 10	110 ,, ... 4 10	110 ,, ... 4 5	Per ton £2 10	Per ton £3 1 0
132 ,, ... 6 3	132 ,, ... 6 3	132 ,, ... 6 3	132 ,, ... 5 11	132 ,, ... 5 0		
154 ,, ... 7 3	154 ,, ... 7 3	154 ,, ... 7 3	154 ,, ... 6 7	154 ,, ... 5 7		
176 ,, ... 8 5	176 ,, ... 8 5	176 ,, ... 8 5	176 ,, ... 7 7	176 ,, ... 6 5		
108 ,, ... 9 7	198 ,, ... 9 7	198 ,, ... 9 7	198 ,, ... 8 5	198 ,, ... 7 3		
220 ,, ... 10 10	220 ,, ... 10 10	220 ,, ... 10 10	220 ,, ... 9 7	220 ,, ... 8 0		

Per ton of 2205 lbs.	Per ton of 2205 lbs.	Per ton of 2205 lbs.	Per ton of 2205 lbs.	Per ton of 2205 lbs.		
Consignments £ s. d. exceeding 220 lbs. but not exceeding 2205 lbs. } 4 0 0	Consignments £ s. d. exceeding 220 lbs., but not exceeding 2205 lbs. } 4 0 0	Consignments £ s. d. exceeding 220 lbs., but not exceeding 2205 lbs. } 4 0 0	Consignments £ s. d. exceeding 220 lbs., but not exceeding 2205 lbs. } 3 4 0	Consignments £ s. d. exceeding 220 lbs. but not exceeding 2205 lbs. } 2 8 2		
Consignments exceeding 2,205 lbs. } 3 16 0	Consignments exceeding 2205 lbs. } 3 16 0	Consignments exceeding 2205 lbs. } 3 16 0	Consignments exceeding 2205 lbs. } 3 4 0	Consignments exceeding 2205 lbs. } 2 8 2		

In addition to the above Rates, a fixed Charge of 2s. 1d. is made on all consignments over 220 lbs.

Rates for Bicycles and Tricycles.

	London to Dieppe.	London to Rouen.	London to Paris.
	s. d.	s. d.	s. d.
Bicycles	6 0	6 10	6 10
Tricycles	12 0	13 8	13 8

Rates for Articles of Value.

	London to Dieppe.	London to Rouen.	London to Paris.
	s. d.	s. d.	s. d.
Gold, Silver, Specie, Jewellery, Precious Stones, Watches, Bills, Bonds, Bank Notes, Securities, Deeds, Bullion, Pictures, Engravings, Statues, Articles of Vertu and Works of Art, per £10 or fraction of £40 declared value.	1 0	1 1	1 4

NOTE—These articles are conveyed by passenger train only, and they must be taxed at the ordinary parcels or grande vitesse rates whenever they are in excess of the value rate.

LONDON TO PARIS,

Via NEWHAVEN, DIEPPE and ROUEN, the SHORTEST and CHEAPEST ROUTE.

WEEK-DAY AND SUNDAY EXPRESS TIDAL SERVICE

This Tidal Service from London to Paris, and *vice versa*, is First, Second and Third Class.

The following **Commodious and Powerful Paddle Steamers**, acknowledged to be the best employed in the Service between England and France, are intended to sail (wind, weather, and other circumstances permitting) between Newhaven and Dieppe, in connection with Special Express and also other Trains between London and Newhaven, and between Dieppe and Paris, as under :—

BRITTANY (Capt. P. Jensen)	BORDEAUX (Capt. P. Jensen)	PARIS (Capt. J. W. Jenkins)
BRIGHTON (Capt. J. S. Clark).	NORMANDY (Capt. H.W. Hemmings)	VICTORIA (Capt. Stubbs).

The New Steamers "NORMANDY" and "BRITTANY" are Steel built and fitted with the Electric Light.

☞ THE TRAINS RUN ALONGSIDE THE STEAMERS BOTH AT NEWHAVEN AND DIEPPE.

PRIVATE CABINS ON BOARD THE STEAMERS.

Quarter Deck Cabins, with two or more berths ; one passenger 20s. per Cabin. | Paddle-box Cabins on S.S. "Paris," "Brighton" and "Victoria," with three
Do.   do.   do.   two or more passengers 30s.   ,, | berths ; one passenger 11s. per Cabin,
| Do.   do.   do.   two or more passengers 16s.   ,,

These Rates to be in addition to the Ordinary Fares between London and Paris.

Second Class Passengers to pay the ordinary change of Cabin Fares *in addition* to the above rates, if they wish to have the privilege of using the Private Cabins.

WEEK-DAY AND SUNDAY EXPRESS TIDAL SERVICE, LONDON TO PARIS.—(1, 2 & 3 CLASS.)

DATES. NOVEMBER, 1886.	Trains leave Victoria.	Trains leave London Bdge.	Steamer leaves Newhaven.	Steamer arrives at Dieppe.	Trains leave Dieppe.	Arrive in Paris.
Monday .... Nov. 1	7 50 p.m.	8 0 p.m.	Nov. 1. 11 0 p.m.	Nov. 2. 4 0 a.m.	5 19 a.m.	9 20 a.m.
Tuesday............ ,, 2	7 50 ,,	8 0 ,,	,, 2. 11 30 ,,	,, 3. 4 30 ,,	5 19 ,,	9 20 ,,
Wednesday......... ,, 3	7 50 ,,	8 0 ,,	,, 4 12 20 a.m.	,, 4. 5 20 ,,	6 12 ,,	10 30 ,,
Thursday .... ,, 4	7 50 ,,	8 0 ,,	,, 5. 1 50 ,,	,, 5. 6 50 ,,	7 27 ,,	11 30 ,,
Friday..... ,, 5	7 50 ,,	8 0 ,,	,, 6. 3 0 ,,	,, 6. 8 0 ,,	9 3 ,,	1 15 p.m.
Saturday............ ,, 6	7 50 ,,	8 0 ,,	,, 6. 10 50 p.m.	,, 7. 5 0 ,,	5 19 ,,	9 20 a.m.
Sunday .... ,, 7	7 50 ,,	8 0 ,,	,, 7. 11 40 ,,	,, 8. 6 0 ,,	6 12 ,,	10 30 ,,
Monday .... ,, 8	7 50 p.m.	8 0 p.m.	,, 9. 12 20 a.m.	,, 9. 6 40 a.m.	7 27 a.m.	11 30 a.m.
Tuesday............ ,, 9	7 50 ,,	8 0 ,,	,, 10. 1 0 ,,	,, 10. 7 10 ,,	7 27 ,,	11 30 ,,
Wednesday .... ,, 10	7 50 ,,	8 0 ,,	,, 11. 1 35 ,,	,, 11. 7 35 ,,	9 3 ,,	1 15 p.m.
Thursday .... ,, 11	7 50 ,,	8 0 ,,	,, 12. 2 10 ,,	,, 12. 8 10 ,,	9 3 ,,	1 15 ,,
Friday............ ,, 12	7 50 ,,	8 0 ,,	,, 13. 2 45 ,,	,, 13. 8 45 ,,	9 3 ,,	1 15 ,,
Saturday......... ,, 13	7 50 ,,	8 0 ,,	,, 14. 3 15 ,,	,, 14. 9 15 ,,	10 25 ,,	2 20 ,,
Sunday .... ,, 14	7 50 ,,	8 0 ,,	,, 15. 3 50 ,,	,, 15. 9 50 ,,	10 1 ,,	2 0 ,,
Monday .... ,, 15	7 50 p.m.	8 0 p.m.	,, 15. 10 45 p.m.	,, 16. 3 45 a.m.	5 19 a.m.	9 20 a.m.
Tuesday............ ,, 16	7 50 ,,	8 0 ,,	,, 16. 11 0 ,,	,, 17. 4 20 ,,	5 19 ,,	9 20 ,,
Wednesday .... ,, 17	7 50 ,,	8 0 ,,	,, 17. 11 0 ,,	,, 18. 4 0 ,,	5 19 ,,	9 20 ,,
Thursday .... ,, 18	7 50 ,,	8 0 ,,	,, 18. 12 0 midt.	,, 19. 5 0 ,,	5 19 ,,	9 20 ,,
Friday .... ,, 19	7 50 ,,	8 0 ,,	,, 20. 1 25 a.m.	,, 20. 6 25 ,,	7 27 ,,	11 30 ,,
Saturday .... ,, 20	7 50 ,,	8 0 ,,	,, 21. 2 50 ,,	,, 21. 7 50 ,,	9 3 ,,	1 15 p.m.
Sunday .... ,, 21	7 50 ,,	8 0 ,,	,, 21. 10 30 p.m.	,, 22. 4 50 ,,	5 19 ,,	9 20 a.m.
Monday .... ,, 22	7 50 p.m.	8 0 p.m.	,, 22. 11 35 p.m.	,, 23. 5 50 a.m.	6 12 a.m.	10 30 a.m.
Tuesday............ ,, 23	7 50 ,,	8 0 ,,	,, 24. 12 25 a.m.	,, 24. 6 40 ,,	7 27 ,,	11 30 ,,
Wednesday......... ,, 24	7 50 ,,	8 0 ,,	,, 25. 1 15 ,,	,, 25. 7 30 ,,	9 3 ,,	1 15 p.m.
Thursday .... ,, 25	7 50 ,,	8 0 ,,	,, 26. 2 0 ,,	,, 26. 8 0 ,,	9 3 ,,	1 15 ,,
Friday............ ,, 26	7 50 ,,	8 0 ,,	,, 27. 2 40 ,,	,, 27. 8 40 ,,	9 3 ,,	1 15 ,,
Saturday .... ,, 27	7 50 ,,	8 0 ,,	,, 28. 3 20 ,,	,, 28. 9 20 ,,	10 1 ,,	2 0 ,,
Sunday .... ,, 28	7 50 ,,	8 0 ,,	,, 28. 10 10 p.m.	,, 29. 3 10 ,,	5 19 ,,	9 20 a.m.
Monday .... ,, 29	7 50 p.m.	8 0 p.m.	,, 29. 10 45 p.m.	,, 30. 3 45 a.m.	5 19 a.m.	9 20 a.m.
Tuesday............ ,, 30	7 50 ,,	8 0 ,,	,, 30. 11 0 ,,	Dec. 1. 4 20 ,,	5 19 ,,	9 20 ,,

---

The London to Newhaven Express Special Trains call at Clapham Junction 8 minutes, East Croydon 32 minutes, Red Hill Junction 52 minutes, and Lewes 1 hour and 38 minutes after leaving Victoria.

☞ To suit the Tides, it may be sometimes necessary for the Boat to leave earlier than the advertised time ; it is therefore necessary for Passengers to be on board the Steamers at least 15 minutes before the advertised sailing, to ensure their not being left behind.

HAVRE, via Newhaven, Dieppe and Rouen.—Passengers are now booked through from London to Havre, and *vice versa* every week-day by this route.

Extract from the LB&SCR Continental Timetable for Nov./Dec. 1886.   *Author's Collection*

LONDON TO PARIS

(Via NEWHAVEN, DIEPPE and ROUEN).

SPECIAL SERVICE

FOR THE CONVEYANCE OF

FISH
LONDON TO PARIS.

(WIND, WEATHER AND OTHER CIRCUMSTANCES PERMITTING.)

TIMES OF DEPARTURE.

DATES. NOVEMBER, 1886.	From LONDON BRIDGE Station.	From LEWES Station.	DATES. DECEMBER, 1886.	From LONDON BRIDGE Station.	From LEWES Station.
Monday .... November 1	6 40 a.m.	8 5 a.m.	Wednesday .... December 1	6 40 a.m.	8 5 a.m.
Tuesday .... ,, 2	6 40 ,,	8 5 ,,	Thursday .... ,, 2	7 50 ,,	10 5 ,,
Wednesday .... ,, 3	7 50 ,,	1 5 ,,	Friday .... ,, 3	7 50 ,,	10 5 ,,
Thursday .... ,, 4	7 50 ,,	10 5 ,,	Saturday .... ,, 4	7 00 ,,	10 5 ,,
Friday .... ,, 5	7 50 ,,	10 5 ,,			
Saturday .... ,, 6	6 40 ,,	8 5 ,,	Monday .... ,, 6	6 40 a.m.	8 5 a.m.
			Tuesday .... ,, 7	6 40 ,,	8 5 ,,
Monday .... ,, 8	7 50 a.m.	10 5 a.m.	Wedne.day .... ,, 8	7 50 ,,	10 5 ,,
Tuesday .... ,, 9	7 50 ,,	10 5 ,,	Thursday .... ,, 9	7 50 ,,	10 5 ,,
Wednesday .... ,, 10	7 50 ,,	10 5 ,,	Friday .... ,, 10	7 50 ,,	10 5 ,,
Thursday .... ,, 11	7 50 ,,	10 5 ,,	Saturday .... ,, 11	7 50 ,,	10 5 ,,
Friday .... ,, 12	7 50 ,,	10 5 ,,			
Saturday .... ,, 13	7 50 ,,	10 5 ,,	Monday .... ,, 13	6 40 a.m.	8 5 a.m.
			Tuesday .... ,, 14	6 40 ,,	8 5 ,,
Monday .... ,, 15	6 40 a.m.	8 5 a.m.	Wednesday .... ,, 15	6 40 ,,	8 5 ,,
Tuesday .... ,, 16	6 40 ,,	8 5 ,,	Thursday .... ,, 16	6 40 ,,	8 5 ,,
Wednesday .... ,, 17	6 40 ,,	8 5 ,,	Friday .... ,, 17	7 50 ,,	10 5 ,,
Thursday .... ,, 18	7 50 ,,	10 5 ,,	Saturday .... ,, 18	7 50 ,,	10 5 ,,
Friday .... ,, 19	7 50 ,,	10 5 ,,			
Saturday .... ,, 20	7 50 ,,	10 5 ,,	Monday .... ,, 20	6 40 a.m.	8 5 a.m.
			Tuesday .... ,, 21	6 40 ,,	8 5 ,,
Monday .... ,, 22	6 40 a.m.	8 5 a.m.	Wednesday .... ,, 22	7 50 ,,	10 5 ,,
Tuesday .... ,, 23	7 50 ,,	10 5 ,,	Thursday .... ,, 23	7 50 ,,	10 5 ,,
Wednesday .... ,, 24	7 50 ,,	10 5 ,,	Friday .... ,, 24	7 50 ,,	10 5 ,,
Thursday .... ,, 25	7 50 ,,	10 5 ,,	Saturday .... ,, 25	NO SERVICE.	
Friday .... ,, 26	7 50 ,,	10 5 ,,			
Saturday .... ,, 27	7 50 ,,	10 5 ,,	Monday .... ,, 27	6 40 a.m.	8 5 a.m.
			Tuesday .... ,, 28	6 40 ,,	8 5 ,,
Monday .... ,, 29	6 40 a.m.	8 5 a.m.	Wednesday .... ,, 29	6 40 ,,	8 5 ,,
Tuesday .... ,, 30	6 40 ,,	8 5 ,,	Thursday .... ,, 30	6 40 ,,	8 5 ,,
			Friday .... ,, 31	6 40 ,,	8 5 ,,

NOTE.

SENDERS are particularly requested to have their consignments delivered at London Bridge at least half-an-hour before the starting of the Trains, otherwise the Companies do not undertake to convey the Goods by this Service.

Extract from the LB&SCR Continental Timetable for Nov./Dec. 1886. *Author's Collection*

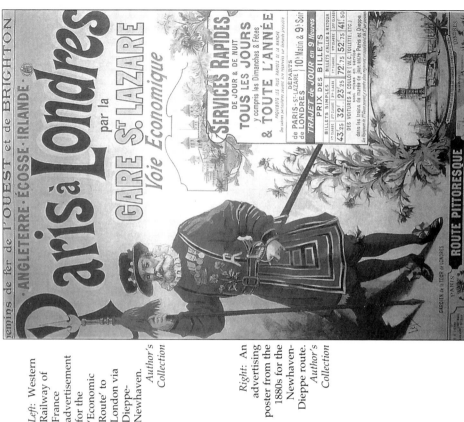

Left: Western Railway of France advertisement for the 'Economic Route' to London via Dieppe-Newhaven.
Author's Collection

Right: An advertising poster from the 1880s for the Newhaven-Dieppe route.
Author's Collection

LONDON & HONFLEUR

(Via NEWHAVEN).

THE SHORTEST AND MOST DIRECT ROUTE (BY NEARLY FORTY MILES) TO TROUVILLE, LISIEUX, CAEN, BAYEAUX, ST. LO, CHERBOURG, ARGENTAN, FALAISE, ALENCON, LE MANS, SILLE-LE-GUILLAUME, LAVAL, VITRE, RENNES, BREST, SABLE, ANGERS, &c., AND THE WEST AND SOUTH-WEST OF FRANCE.

Honfleur is in Direct Communication with Havre by Steamers twice a day, 30 minutes' passage, First Class, 10d., Second Class, 5d. The Steamers "HONFLEUR," "RENNES," "VIKING," and "IDA," are appointed to sail with Passengers and Merchandise (weather and unavoidable circumstances permitting), from the NEWHAVEN QUAY for HONFLEUR, and *vice versa*, as under:—

LONDON TO HONFLEUR.

DATES. November, 1886.		Trains leave		Steamer leaves New- haven Harbour.	DATES. December, 1886.		Trains leave		Steamer leaves New- haven Harbour.
		Victoria Station.	London Bridge.				Victoria Station.	London Bridge.	
Wednesday	Nov. 3	1 30 p.m.	2 5 p.m.	4 0 p.m.	Wednesday	Dec. 1	10 5 a.m.	9 45 a.m.	1 0 p.m.
Saturday	,, 6	4 30 ,,	5 5 ,,	7 0 ,,	Saturday	,, 4	1 30 p.m.	2 5 p.m.	4 0 ,,
Wednesday	,, 10	7 50 p.m.	8 0 p.m.	10 0 p.m.	Wednesday	,, 8	7 50 p.m.	8 0 p.m.	10 0 p.m.
Saturday	,, 13	7 50 ,,	8 0 ,,	12 0 mdt.	Saturday	,, 11	7 50 ,,	8 0 ,,	10 0 ,,
Wednesday	,, 17	10 5 a.m.	9 45 a.m.	1 0 p.m.	Wednesday	,, 15	10 5 a.m.	9 45 a.m.	1 0 p.m.
Saturday	,, 20	4 30 p.m.	5 5 p.m.	7 0 ,,	Saturday	,, 18	1 30 p.m.	2 5 p.m.	4 0 ,,
Wednesday	,, 24	7 50 p.m.	8 0 p.m.	10 0 p.m.	Wednesday	,, 22	7 50 p.m.	8 0 p.m.	10 0 p.m.
Saturday	,, 27	7 50 ,,	8 0 ,,	12 0 mdt.	Sunday	,, 26	7 0 a.m.	7 25 a.m.	10 0 a.m.
					Wednesday	,, 29	10 5 ,,	9 45 ,,	1 0 p.m.

HONFLEUR TO LONDON.

Dates, November, 1886.		Steamer leaves Honfleur.	DATES, December, 1886.		Steamer leaves Honfleur.	TRAINS LEAVE NEWHAVEN HARBOUR FOR LONDON AS UNDER.	
						WEEK DAYS.	SUNDAYS AND CHRISTMAS DAY.
Tuesday	Nov. 2	1 0 p.m.	Wednesday	Dec. 1	12 0 midt.		
Wednesday	,, 3	2 0 ,,	Friday	,, 3	2 0 p.m.	6 55 a.m.	7 49 a.m.
Friday	,, 5	3 0 ,,	Saturday	,, 4	3 0 ,,	8 55 ,,	5 58 p.m.
Saturday	,, 6	5 0 ,,	Monday	,, 6	5 0 ,,	10 53 ,,	
			Wednesday	,, 8	7 0 ,,	2 30 p.m.	
Monday	,, 8	6 0 p.m.	Friday	,, 10	8 0 ,,	4 10 ,,	
Wednesday	,, 10	7 0 ,,	Saturday	,, 11	8 30 ,,	5 40 ,,	
Friday	,, 12	8 0 ,,	Monday	,, 13	10 0 p.m.	7 42 ,,	
Saturday	,, 13	9 0 ,,	Tuesday	,, 14	10 0 ,,		
			Wednesday	,, 15	11 0 ,,	Third Class Passengers can only	
Monday	,, 15	11 0 p.m.	Thursday	,, 16	12 0 midt.	travel by Third Class trains.	
Wednesday	,, 17	12 0 midt.	Friday	,, 17	1 0 p.m.		
Friday	,, 19	2 0 p.m.	Saturday	,, 18	12 0 midt.	VICTORIA STATION.—For the	
Saturday	,, 20	3 0 ,,	Monday	,, 20	4 0 p.m.	convenience of Passengers, a Lavatory	
			Tuesday	,, 21	5 0 ,,	and Dressing Room, with Toilet and	
Monday	,, 22	6 0 p.m.	Wednesday	,, 22	6 0 ,,	Travelling conveniences, have been pro-	
Wednesday	,, 24	7 0 ,,	Thursday	,, 23	7 0 ,,	vided at the Victoria Station.	
Friday	,, 26	8 0 ,,	Monday	,, 27	9 0 p.m.	HOTEL AT LONDON BRIDGE.—	
Saturday	,, 27	9 0 ,,	Wednesday	,, 29	11 0 ,,	For convenience of Travellers by this	
			Friday	,, 31	12 0 midt.	Route, a commodious and comfortable	
Monday	,, 29	11 0 p.m.				Hotel at moderate charges is now con-	
						nected (under cover) with the Railway	
						Station at London Bridge.	

The Company reserves to itself the right to postpone the Saturday departures from Honfleur, to Sunday.

Special Cheap Return Tickets, available for one week, are issued from Brighton, Worthing, Littlehampton, Chichester, Havant, Portsmouth, to Honfleur. Fares—First Class, **20s.** ; Second Class, **15s.** ; Third Class, **10s.**

Passengers Booked Through to Honfleur.—Passengers can be booked from Brighton, Portsmouth, Havant, Chichester, Worthing, Midhurst, Dorking, Leatherhead, Epsom, Hastings, St. Leonards, Eastbourne, Tunbridge Wells, Red Hill Junction, Croydon, Norwood Junction, Kensington, Clapham Juncti·n, 23, Black Prince, Piccadilly, No. 8, Grand Hotel Buildings, Trafalgar Square, and 18, Fish Street Hill, at the same Fares as the London Termini. Passengers from or to London may break their journey at Brighton or Newhaven.

Return Tickets Extended.—Tickets can be made available to return at a later date on payment of 10 per cent. of cost of Ticket for the first fortnight or portion thereof, and 5 per cent. extra for each week or portion of a week after the first fortnight, such payment being made before the date of expiry of the Ticket and at the Station from which the journey is to be completed.

Luggage can now be registered throughout from London on payment of 6d. 66 lbs. allowed Free to each Passenger; any excess above that weight charged for at ½d. per lb.

The Trains between London and Newhaven are fitted with a communication between Passenger, Guard, and Driver, and are provided with the Westinghouse Continuous Automatic Brake.

Trains from Honfleur to Trouville, Bayeaux, Caen, Cherbourg, &c.—Trains each way daily between these places, and also to and from other places in the West and South West of France as above.

Special Steamers.—All particulars as to charges for Special Boats can be obtained on application at London Bridge and Victoria Stations, and at the City and West End Offices, 18, Fish Street Hill, London. All goods should be directed in full, as follows: " To HONFLEUR. via NEWHAVEN, per LONDON BRIGHTON AND SOUTH COAST RAILWAY," and may be delivered at the Thames Junction Wharf, Deptford, or can be carted in by the Railway Company at very moderate rates.

Parcels and Light Goods only can be delivered at the London and Brighton Company's Receiving Offices; 33, Cannon Street, E.C. ; 69, Old Bailey, E.C.; 452, Strand, W.C.; 28, Regent Circus, Piccadilly, W.; New White Horse Cellar, 67, Piccadilly, W.; St. Thomas' Street, Borough, and at Victoria Station.

There are no Pier Dues or Clearing Charges at Newhaven.

For further particulars apply at the General Offices at the LONDON BRIDGE and VICTORIA TERMINI, also GOODS DEPOT, WILLOW WALK, BERMONDSEV, and 28, REGENT CIRCUS, PICCADILLY; No. 8, GRAND HOTEL BUILDINGS, Trafalgar Square ; or at any Station on the London Brighton and South Coast Railway.

HONFLEUR, F. LETHRIDGE, Quai de Quarai tine.

NEWHAVEN (SUSSEX), The Company's Wharfinger Railway Wharf.

VITRE, M. PARMENTIER, Correspondent of Western Railway of France.

CAEN, F. LETHRIDGE, Rue des Carmes, 66.

HAVRE, CHARLES AUNE, Quai de l'Ile.

TROUVILLE, DEAUVILLE, M. HERBERT, Courtier Maritime.

LE MANS, M. CRUCHON MIGNON, 25 bis, Rue Coeffort.

And at the other Stations on the Western of France Railway.

Extract from the LB&SCR Continental Timetable for Nov./Dec. 1886.   *Author's Collection*

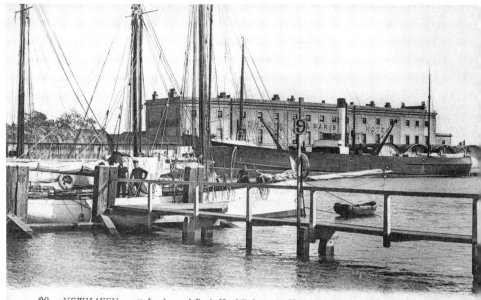

20   NEWHAVEN. — " London and Paris-Hotel " from the Harbour. — LL.

The cargo vessel *Caen* joined the fleet in 1890 under the French flag. It was powered by twin triple expansion engines rated at 115 hp.   *Author's Collection*

Berthed at the Quai Henri IV, Dieppe, is the SS *Tamise*. This French-crewed passenger ferry was built by the Forges et Chantiers de la Mediteranee at Havre in 1893.   *Author's Collection*

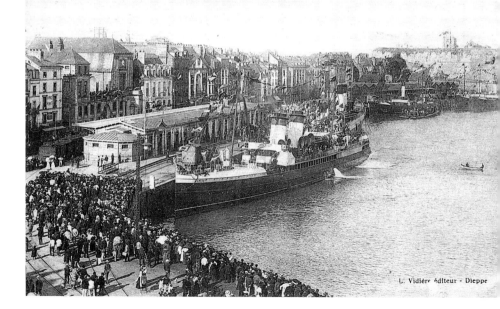

L. Vidière Aditeur - Dieppe

Following the completion of the dredging programmes at Newhaven and Dieppe the joint service announced that from 1st April, 1889 the first 'Fixed Timetable Service' would begin. This new non-tidal service greatly simplified the timetabling of connecting trains from, and to, London and Paris. The old PS *Rouen* (I) was sold out of the fleet having now been replaced, the next year saw the demise of the PS *Bordeaux*. Two new vessels joined the fleet in 1890, they were the sister ships TSS *Angers* and TSS *Caen*. These vessels were built for the French partners at Le Havre for cargo service. They were 210 ft long, 26 ft wide and had a gross tonnage of 522 tons. Each was powered by twin triple expansion engines which produced a maximum output of 115 hp.

PS *Paris* (I) was involved an incident during a passage from Dieppe when a north-westerly gale turned into a full blown blizzard and heavy seas pounded the ship. In mid-channel the starboard paddle was damaged and the engines had to be shut down. The vessel drifted helplessly with only the aid of a sea anchor to give some stability. After several hours the *Emerald* a cargo ship, came upon the drifting ship and with great difficulty attached a tow line to her which held for only two hours before parting. The two vessels lost sight of each other in the mountainous seas and they drifted apart. Off Cape Gris Nez the *Paris* suddenly took on a list to port and the Captain, Capt. Sharp, correctly assumed that the damaged part of the paddle had fallen off and the engines were restarted. Under reduced power she crept towards Dover where she made port 36 hours after her departure from Dieppe. The LBSCR rewarded the Captain and Chief Engineer with inscribed watches and the entire crew were given an extra month's pay; the passengers, grateful for their lives, also made presentations.

The work on the breakwater at Newhaven, begun in 1878, was finally completed in 1891 and the entrance to the port was now made safe in all weathers. Another building project was also completed this year when the North Quay was opened specifically for the importation of timber from the Baltic.

The TSS *Seine* joined the fleet in 1891, being the first passenger vessel to be built in France for the joint company. She was also the first passenger ship to be manned by a French crew following a change to the crewing arrangement. From now on French and English crews would share the passenger and cargo duties. TSS *Seine* was built at Le Havre by Forges et Chantiers and was 269 ft long, 30 ft wide and her triple expansion engines produced 307 hp. On 8th August TSS *Seine* made the cross-channel trip in only three hours and 11 minutes. The following year the PS *Marseilles* retired from the fleet.

The year 1893 saw the introduction of year-round day services which were restricted to 1st and 2nd class passengers only, 3rd class having to travel by night to make space for the increasing passenger requirements. A second French passenger vessel joined the fleet this year, she was the TSS *Tamise*. Although nominally a sister ship of the TSS *Seine* her upperworks were quite different and she was fitted with a pair of ugly funnels with strange straw boater-like caps on the top. PS *Brighton* suffered an unfortunate accident in Dieppe harbour when she struck a pier and sank in shallow water. No lives were lost and the vessel was refloated, however, she was sold shortly afterwards.

The harbour at Caen. The LBSCR ran cargo vessels to this port from both Littlehampton and Newhaven.   *Author's Collection*

An Edwardian view of the Quai Henri IV at Dieppe showing the TrSS *Brighton* alongside the Gare Maritime. This station was built in 1900 to replace the old wooden sheds used previously.   *Author's Collection*

151   DIEPPE. — Le Train de Paris et la Malle. — LL.

The fleet increased in size quite sharply in 1894 with the introduction of four new vessels. A dredger, the SS *Leven*, was purchased second-hand, she was originally built in 1885 at Renfrew and was 185 ft long and 28 ft wide in the beam. TSS *Seaford* was built by Denny Bros of Dumbarton, following an order placed in August 1893. She was equipped with four triple expansion engines producing 292 hp and a top speed of about 20 knots. Some 257 ft long and 34 ft wide, TSS *Seaford* had a single funnel and one raked back mast forward. Her time with the fleet was cut short when on 20th August, 1895, returning from Dieppe in bad weather and thick fog, she was about 20 miles out from Newhaven and collided with another of the company's vessels, the TSS *Lyon*. *Seaford* came off the worst in the encounter and began taking on water immediately. Passengers from the stricken ship were transferred to *Lyon* which had come alongside, 250 in all were saved. *Seaford* sank shortly afterwards and *Lyon* returned to Newhaven. At the subsequent enquiry the master of the *Lyon* was found to be at fault. The other two new vessels in 1894 were the sister ships TSS *Calvados* (I) and TSS *Trouville* (I); these two cargo ships were built by Denny's of Dumbarton for the LBSCR's sole use on the Newhaven-Caen route. Twin-screwed, they were powered by triple expansion machinery producing 104 hp. In 1901 both vessels were exchanged with the South Eastern and Chatham Railway, *Calvados* was immediately resold to the General Steam Navigation Company and renamed *Alouette*, she was broken up at Rainham in 1924. *Trouville* was retained by the SECR but renamed *Walmer*, surviving until 1935 when she was scrapped.

By 1895 the old cargo vessel SS *Viking* was becoming past her best, and so after 24 years she was sold. A new steam launch, *Sultan*, was purchased this year. Her main duties were to potter about the port of Newhaven and deliver stores and messages to the companies ships in the harbour at the time. TSS *Prince Arthur* was built for the LBSCR's Newhaven-Caen route by Denny's, although similar in design to *Calvados* and *Trouville* she was 10 tons heavier. It had sleeping accommodation for 28 first class passengers on sofa beds covered in Utrecht velvet. A ladies' saloon had 24 sofa beds fitted, all saloons and cabins were lined with pine. TSS *Prince Arthur* was also exchanged with the SECR in 1901. Following the demise of the short-lived *Seaford* in 1895 a replacement was urgently required. The TSS *Sussex* (II) made her maiden voyage on 31st July, 1896, built, as so many of her predecessors had been, by Denny's she was almost identical to her sister *Seaford* but was 12 ft longer. By 1897 the passenger fleet had to cope with an increasing number of travellers, and so the capacity had to be increased yet again. The French partners added the TSS *Manche* to the passenger fleet list, she was similar to the TSS *Tamise* of 1893 with the same straw boater funnels.

In 1898 the Royal Mail was carried on the Newhaven-Dieppe route for the first time, providing a bonus for the owners in added revenue and for the passengers there was a stricter adherence to the timetable to comply with the Postmaster General's rules. By 1899 the LBSCR had passed its probationary period without serious delay to the mail and was allowed by the PMG to fly the Royal Mail pennant from the masthead of any vessel employed in the carriage of mail.

The SS *Trouville*, 1894, was involved in a bizarre ship swap in 1901. The LBSCR exchanged three new vessels; *Trouville*, *Calvados* and *Prince Arthur* for two old cargo ships owned by the SE&CR.
B. Cakebread

An unusual rear view of the SS *Sussex* showing the steering gear. *Sussex* was launched in 1896 as an urgent replacement for the *Seaford* which had sunk the previous year. *Author's Collection*

Built in 1896 the SS *Prince Arthur* was a passenger/cargo vessel on the Newhaven-Caen route. The *Prince Arthur* was exchanged with the SE&CR in 1901. *Author's Collection*

The SS *Manche*, launched in 1897, was virtually identical to the *Tamise* of 1893. Seen entering Dieppe she shows the flags which were a code to warn the quayside workers how many passengers of each class to expect. *Author's Collection*

Launched in 1899 the TSS *France* suffered a terrible accident shortly after entering service, nine members of the boiler room staff were scalded to death when a steam pipe burst.

Author's Collection

Built by Denny's of Dumbarton for the LBSCR, the *Arundel* was fast and sumptuously decorated. The first class smoking room, for example, was upholstered in buffalo hide and panelled in mahogany.

Author's Collection

The old SS *Newhaven* (I) was sold in 1899 after 24 years service, and the cargo vessel SS *Angers* was also disposed of, not because of age but because it was involved in an accident. Whilst entering Dieppe harbour in a heavy sea she began to take on water and sank, the wreck being disposed of locally as scrap. Another new French vessel was commissioned for the fleet in 1899. The TSS *France* built at Le Havre, followed the French tradition of being functional without being beautiful. She had two ugly, squat, funnels and a whaleback deck forward. Whilst under the builder's guarantee she suffered a burst steam pipe and nine of the engine room staff were scalded to death.

With 1900 came a new century and three more new vessels built for the fleet. They were the TSS *Brest* (I), TSS *Cherbourg* and the TSS *Arundel*. The first two were cargo vessels identical in design and were built by the Societe des Forges et Chantiers de la Mediteranee at Le Havre for the Western Railway of France. TSS *Arundel* was built for the LBSCR by Denny's of Dumbarton, and this passenger ship had four-cylinder triple expansion engines capable of a top speed of 20½ knots. The specification to the builders stated that the 1st class smoking room on the promenade deck should be upholstered in Buffalo hide, framed in teak and panelled in mahogany. The rest of the ship was as sumptuously appointed. Travellers at Dieppe received new accommodation this year, the Ouest building a new station at the Gare Maritime, finally replacing the old wooden sheds built in 1874.

The year 1901 saw a flurry of activity on the fleet list with no fewer than 10 vessels changing hands. As previously mentioned the TSS *Calvados* (I), TSS *Trouville* (I) and TSS *Prince Arthur* were exchanged with the South Eastern Railway for the SS *Roubaix* (1874) and the SS *Paris* (1878); one hopes that the cash settlement was heavily in favour of the LBSCR. Once in Brighton hands the boats were quickly renamed SS *Trouville* (II) and SS *Calvados* (II) respectively, and served on the LBSCR's Newhaven-Caen route. The PS *Brittany* and the French-owned vessel SS *Dieppe* (II) were also sold out of the fleet. The only new vessel to join the fleet was the tug *Alert*.

Between 1901 and 1913 the LBSCR purchased a total of seven coal lighters to carry bunker fuel to refuel vessels at Newhaven. The first two were built at Newhaven, the next two at Littlehampton and the final three at Southampton, Seaford and Portsmouth respectively. Average dimensions for all vessels were 65 ft long, 20 ft wide, a depth of 6 ft and a weight of around 57 tons. Un-named or numbered by the LBSCR all survived into the Southern Railway era, being numbered SR9 to SR14, there being two number 10s.

With the arrival of *Alert*, tug *Pinafore* was surplus to requirements and so she was sold in 1901. Two other vessels to be paid off were the *Normandy* (II)) and the *Brittany*, both built in 1882. These were sold to the Liverpool and Douglas Steamers Ltd (L&DSL) in 1902. The L&DSL were at that time involved in a battle for passengers with the Isle of Man Steam Packet Co., a battle the Liverpool company failed to win.

In 1902 the TSS *Portsmouth* joined the fleet, she was another cargo vessel and was a sister of *Brest* and *Cherbourg* of 1900. The following year the LBSCR received its first turbine steamer, the TrSS *Brighton* (IV). Built in Scotland by Denny's of Dumbarton its Parsons triple turbines produced 6,000 hp, driving the ship along at

In 1902 the French partners added another cargo vessel to the fleet, she was the SS *Portsmouth*. 204 ft long and 26 ft wide her engines produced up to 560 hp at top speed.   *L. Marshall*

The French cargo vessel SS *Portsmouth*, 1902, tied up to the station wharf at Newhaven.
B. Cakebread

THE SEINE

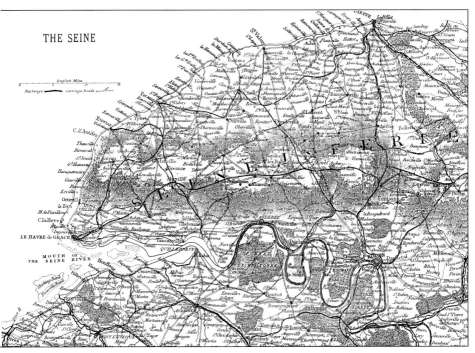

The Seine.   *Reproduced from Black's Guide, 1908*

Dieppe.   *Reproduced from Black's Guide, 1908*

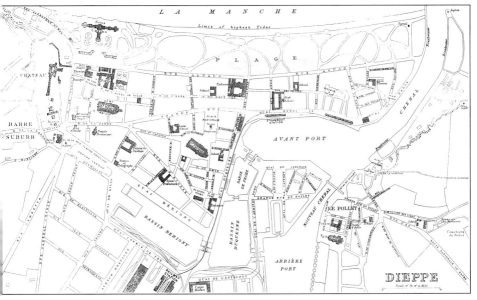

Above: With a top speed of 21.37 knots the TrSS *Brighton*, 1901, was put to good use during World War I. Seen here in its guise as a hospital ship having been commandeered by the Admiralty for the duration of the war.
Author's Collection

Right: This LBSCR official postcard view shows the plush accommodation to be found in a first class Ladies Boudoir on board the TrSS *Brighton* of 1901.
Author's Collection

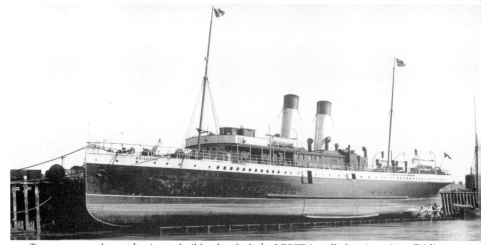

To save money by not having to build a dry dock the LBSCR installed an ingenious Gridiron at Newhaven. The vessel to be worked on, in this case TrSS *Brighton*, was floated on at high tide and then as the tide receded the hull was left high and dry enabling light repairs to be carried out.   *L. Marshall*

a top speed of 21.37 knots. *Rouen* (III) was sold to Messrs Little of Barrow in Furness and renamed *Duchess of Buccleuch*. The same year (1903) saw the joint company receiving its licence to transmit messages by wireless telegraphy, as developed by Marconi, and the following year WT stations were set up at Newhaven and Dieppe. The second steam turbine vessel joined the fleet in 1905, she was TrSS *Dieppe* (IV), built by Fairfield and Co. of Glasgow, her engines producing a top speed of 21.64 knots. Another new addition in this year was the tug *Hauler*; 1905 also saw the sale of the dredger *Leven*, and the following year the TSS *Seine* was sold.

The years 1907-09 were unusually stable for the fleet list with no new vessels and no withdrawals. In 1909 the French partner was nationalised and with others was renamed ETAT, or French State Railways. Following the lull in shipbuilding there was a flurry of activity in 1910 with no fewer than six new vessels joining the fleet. The first two vessels were non-revenue earning coal lighters; not named by the LBSCR they became SR10 and SR11 in 1923. SS *Normandy* (III) and SS *Brittany* (II) were cargo vessels built by Earle and Co. of Hull for the Newhaven-Caen via Ouistreham Canal route. The last pair of vessels were French additions, the TSS *Anjou* and the TSS *Maine*, built by Ateliers et Chantiers de la Loire at St Nazaire. Both were designed for cargo duties between the coast of France and Newhaven. After 25 years of service the *Italie* was finally retired.

At 4.30 pm on Sunday 6th November, 1910 the TrSS *Brighton* was in collision with the sailing vessel *Preussen*. *Brighton* under command of Captain Hemmings, had just left Newhaven *en route* for Dieppe when in heavy seas she tried to cross in front of *Preussen*. The two ships collided and *Brighton* tore a 15 ft gash in *Preussen's* bow, smashed the bowsprit and brought down most of the sailing ship's top hamper. Captain Hemmings turned about and returned to Newhaven to raise the alarm. The tug *Alert* went out and managed to get a line on the *Preussen* and take her in tow for the harbour; unfortunately *Preussen* was driven aground under the South Foreland Rocks and was a total loss. At the subsequent inquiry Captain Hemmings was found to be solely at fault for the accident.

More movements in the shipping lists occurred in 1911 when three old vessels were retired, these being the *Calvados*, *Trouville* and *Lyons*. *Lyons* was sold to the British Salvage Association Ltd, a consortium formed to attempt to raise the treasure of the *Lutine* which sank in 1799 carrying a 1910 estimate of £1.5 million in gold bullion. The *Lutine*, whose famous ship's bell is rung in Lloyds of London when a vessel is reported as lost, sunk off the Dutch coast near to the island of Terschelling in 10 metres of shifting mud. Fitted with powerful suction apparatus, *Lyons* was moored for three years over the wreck but managed to recover only a handful of gold and silver coins, 15 cannons, two anchors and various pieces of scrap metal. The sale of this treasure raised the princely sum of £135, which barely covered running costs for three months!

The first French-produced turbine ship joined the fleet in 1911, she was the TrSS *Newhaven* (III). Built by Forges et Chantiers in Havre, *Newhaven*, along with her sister TrSS *Rouen* (V), launched in 1912, had direct-coupled Parsons' turbines which produced 7,500 bhp and a top speed of 15 knots. Also joining the fleet in 1912 was the TSS *Bordeaux* this was a sister ship to the cargo vessels *Anjou* and *Maine* and was built by Ateliers et Chantiers of St Nazaire. The Newhaven-Caen

London Brighton & South Coast
. . AND .
Western of France Railways

PARIS _{AND THE} CONTINENT

TWO EXPRESS SERVICES DAILY.
FAST STEAMERS AND CORRIDOR TRAINS.

TO FRANCE, ITALY, SWITZERLAND
AND AUSTRIA.

CYCLING & MOTORING IN NORMANDY.

Dieppe (5 hours from London) is the best and most popular starting point for Cycling and Motoring Tours in Normandy.

EXCELLENT ROADS AND SCENERY.

Full particulars of Fares and Services of

CONTINENTAL TRAFFIC MANAGER

L.B.& S.C.Rly. London Bridge Terminus

Edwardian advertisement for the LBSCR's Continental Services.   *Author's Collection*

MOTOR
ᘓ CARS
VIA NEWHAVEN
AND
DIEPPE.

SHIPPING MOTOR CAR AT NEWHAVEN.

MOTOR CARS, when accompanied by the owners or their representatives, can be shipped, weather and other circumstances permitting, on the passenger boats sailing between Newhaven and Dieppe. For further particulars write or telephone (Westminster 874) to the Continental Manager, Brighton Railway, Victoria Station, S.W., stating date of proposed journey, weight of car, and whether it is desired to cross by the day or night Passenger Boat.

RATES. - The rates for the conveyance of accompanied Motor Cars from Newhaven to Dieppe and vice versa are as follows.—

Motor Cars with wheel-base less
than 6ft. 4in.
{ £3 10 0 per Car.
{ £2 10 0 per Car at Owner's Risk.

„   „   6ft. 4in. to 8ft. 4in.
{ £4 5 0 per Car.
{ £3 0 0 per Car at Owner's Risk.

„   „   8ft. 4in. to 10ft. 4in.
{ £5 0 0 per Car.
{ £3 10 0 per Car at Owner's Risk.

„   „   exceeding 10ft. 4in.
{ £5 16 0 per Car.
{ £4 0 0 per Car at Owner Risk.

By the term wheel-base is meant the distance between the axles, measured from the points where the front and back wheels touch the ground immediately below the centres of the axles, those being at the time parallel to each other, and in taking the measurement, care should be exercised to see that the front and rear axles are exactly parallel to each other. In case of doubt, the distance would be measured on each side of the Car and the average taken as the required measurement.

The only additional charges are for French Government Stamp, &c., viz., on Cars shipped from Newhaven to Dieppe 1.- and from Dieppe to Newhaven 1/11.

Cars for shipment at Newhaven by the Passenger Boats should reach the port at least 1 hour before the time fixed for the departure of the Boats. At Dieppe, Cars for shipment by the **DAY** Passenger Boats should reach the port at least 1½ hours prior to the hour of sailing; if for shipment by the **NIGHT** Passenger Boats, Cars can be accepted up to midnight if accompanied by a "Tryptique" or deposit voucher, but failing the possession of either of these documents, they should reach Dieppe by 5.0 p.m.

GARAGES, SUPPLY OF PETROL, &c., at NEWHAVEN and DIEPPE.— Arrangements have been made both at Newhaven and Dieppe to enable Motor Car owners to obtain a supply of petrol immediately their Cars are landed from the boats.

At NEWHAVEN.—Messrs. J. Amy & Sons, 1, Norton Road, the Agents of the Royal Automobile Club, and Messrs. French & Co., 37, High Street, who represent the Automobile Association and Motor Union, attend the arrival of all boats, and, in addition to supplying petrol, are prepared to render assistance to Motorists.

At DIEPPE.—Monsieur Ch. Meyer, Place de Casino, represents the Royal Automobile Club and the Automobile Association and Motor Union, and the Automobile Co-operative Association, Limited, and is always ready to render any assistance and supply petrol to motorists arriving by boat from Newhaven. An interpreter of the French State Railways is also stationed at the Gare Maritime to render every assistance in the clearance of Cars through the Customs.

INSURANCE.—On instructions being given by the sender on his declaration, the Insurance of Motor Cars against sea and all other transit risks can be effected by the Companies at Lloyd's at a premium of 2s. 5d. per £40 or fraction of £40 value. The actual value of the cars to be insured must be declared by the Owners at the time of forwarding if they wish to be fully compensated in case of loss. [Continued on next page.

Extract from the LB&SCR Continental Timetable for Winter 1911-1912. *Author's Collection*

LONDON AND CAEN (Via NEWHAVEN AND OUISTREHAM CANAL.)

THE ONLY DIRECT ROUTE TO CAEN.

The Direct Route for TROUVILLE, CABOURG, LUC-SUR-MER, HONFLEUR, CHERBOURG, LISIEUX, ARGENTAN, LE MANS, TOURS, ANGERS, GRANVILLE, and all parts of LOWER NORMANDY and UPPER BRITTANY.

The new Steamers " Normandy " and " Brittany " are appointed to sail (weather and unavoidable circumstances permitting) from Newhaven to Caen, and vice versa :—

For list of Passenger and Cargo Sailings, see Small Bills.

PASSENGER FARES.

SINGLE, available day of issue only. Return Journey Tickets not issued.

No reduction can be made on the Boat for a child, but two children under 12 years of age may travel with one adult Ticket.

			s.	d.
LONDON TO CAEN or vice versâ, 1st Class Rail and Saloon	... ...	24	6
Do. do. 2nd Class Rail and Saloon	... ...	20	8
Do. do. 3rd Class Rail and Saloon	... ...	19	5
NEWHAVEN TO CAEN or vice versâ, Saloon	... ...	15	0
PRIVATE CABIN.—One Passenger	... ...	10s.	
Two Passengers	... ...	15s.	

In addition to Saloon Fares.

IMPORTANT NOTICE.—Only a limited number of passengers are carried by these Steamers, and it is therefore advisable, to avoid disappointment, to book as early as possible in advance, tickets being only issued (without previous notice), up to the number available, at Victoria and Newhaven Harbour for the voyage from Newhaven, and at Caen (38, Rue Gilbert) for the return journey. Passengers for England are allowed to embark at Ouistreham, providing they have previously taken a ticket or if there is accommodation available.

BAGGAGE.—Each Adult Saloon or First Class Passenger is allowed 120* lbs., and each Child 60*lbs. of Baggage free between Newhaven and Caen and between London and Caen, and a charge of 1s. 0d. per Passenger is made for registration. Excess Baggage is charged at the rate of 6d. between Newhaven and Caen, and 11d. between London and Caen for every 10 lbs. or part of 10 lbs. The Customs examination will be made at Caen on the outward journey and at Newhaven on the homeward journey, and Passengers must be present at this operation. Passengers are allowed to take Baggage on shore at Ouistreham providing it contains nothing dutiable.

In the case of Passengers taking Second Class or Third Class Rail Tickets between London and Newhaven and requiring to register their Baggage through, the allowance is reduced to 100 lbs. and 60 lbs. respectively for an Adult, and to 50 lbs. and 30 lbs. for a Child.

The Company will not be responsible for any luggage except that of the description mentioned in their Acts of Parliament, unless the same is booked and paid for according to its value and a Description of its nature made at the time of booking, and even when booked no responsibility is incurred by the Company for any damage arising from accident of the sea, nor in any case for a greater sum than £10 for any one package.

RATES FOR BICYCLES, TRICYCLES, MOTOR CYCLES, &c., when accompanied by Passengers.

London & Caen. Newhaven & Caen. At Owner's Risk.

		London & Caen		Newhaven & Caen	
		s.	d.	s.	d.
Bicycles, Perambulators and Mail Carts ...	each	4	0	2	6
Cycle Trailers ...	,,	5	6	2	6
Children's Folding Chairs and Mail Carts (not exceeding 20 lbs.)	,,	2	3	1	6
Tandems and Triplet Bicycles	,,	7	0	4	0
Tricycles, and Bicycles to carry more than three persons; Bath Chairs and Invalid Carrying Chairs	,,	8	0	5	0
Motor Bicycles (not exceeding 120 lbs.)	,,	7	0 (a)	4	0 (a)
Motor cycles with three or more wheels to carry one person (not exceeding 200 lbs.)	,,	13	6 (a)	7	6 (a)
Motor Cycles with three or more wheels to carry two persons (not exceeding 300 lbs.)	,,	20	0 (a)	12	0 (a)

(a) 6d. between Newhaven and Caen and 11d. between London and Caen will be charged in addition for every 10 lbs. or part of 10 lbs. in excess of the weight named.

RATES FOR HORSES, CARRIAGES AND DOGS.

	London and Caen s. d.	Newhaven and Caen s. d.		London and Caen s. d.	Newhaven and Caen s. d.
*Horses (not exceeding £50 value)	60 0	45 0	Carriages, two wheels ...	45 0	35 0
*Ponies under 12 hands (not exceeding £25 value) ...	50 0	30 0	Carriages, four wheels ...	60 0	47 6
*Mules (not exceeding £5 value) ...	50 0	30 0	Motor Cars (unpacked) ...	60 0	47 6
			Dogs (not exceeding £2 value) ...	5 0	4 0

* See Notice on page 117.

PARCELS BY GRANDE VITESSE.

Not exceeding	7 lbs.	14 lbs.	28 lbs.	56 lbs.	84 lbs.	112 lbs.	& above.
	s. d.	s. d.	s. d.	s. d.	s. d.	s. d.	s. d.
London and Caen	1 3	1 9	2 3	2 9	3 3	4 3	4 3 per cwt.

PARCELS AND SMALLS BY PETITE VITESSE.

Not exceeding	7 lbs.	14 lbs.	28 lbs.	Over 28 lbs. until more at tonnage rate.
	s. d.	s. d.	s. d.	s. d.
London and Caen	1 0	1 6	2 0	2 6
Newhaven and Caen	0 9	1 0	1 6	2 0

FISH, FRUIT, MEAT, POULTRY AND VEGETABLES PER GRANDE VITESSE.

	Per Ton. s. d.		Per Ton. s. d.
London and Caen...	50 0	Newhaven and Caen	30 0
,, ,, ,, (at Owner's risk) ...	45 0		

NOTE.—The London rates apply to any station on the London Brighton and South Coast Railway.

For full particulars see Special Bills, or apply to—
NEWHAVEN (Sussex) Wharf Superintendent, Harbour Station.
CAEN—Mr. Henry M. Hardy, 38, Rue Guilbert.—Telegrams : " Markhardy, Caen,"
LE MANS—Mr. L. Mahoudeau, 11, Rue Pere Mersenne.
LONDON—Continental Traffic Manager, Brighton Railway, Victoria, S.W.

Extract from the LB&SCR Continental Timetable for Winter 1911-1912. *Author's Collection*

This general seaward view of Newhaven Harbour shows on the left *Dieppe* on the Gridiron, and
Sleepers Hollow and Newhaven Fort on the right of the harbour mouth.   *Author's Collection*

The first French steam turbine vessel was the TrSS *Newhaven*. She was launched in 1911 and her
direct-coupled triple expansion engines produced 7,500 hp, but a surprisingly slow top speed of
only 15 knots.   *Author's Collection*

474 — DIEPPE. Le Paquebot « Newhaven » quittant le Quai. ND Phot.

The harbour mouth at Newhaven. The 2,800 yard mole was built between 1878 and 1891 to protect the harbour entrance from storms during the frequent winter easterly winds.

Author's Collection

Newhaven Harbour viewed from Sleepers Hole. In the foreground are three of the LBSCR's coal lighters. Tied up in the middle ground are, *left to right*; *Paris*, *Dieppe* and *Manche*.

Author's Collection

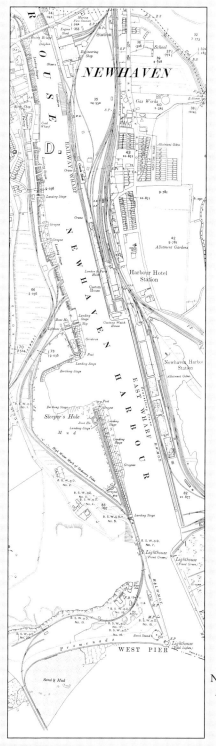

Newhaven Harbour.
Reproduced from the 25", 1910
Ordnance Survey Map

An aerial view of Newhaven Harbour from the sea. On the left, front to rear are: Newhaven Fort, Sleepers Hollow and Newhaven Town. On the right, front to rear are: East Wharf and Railway Wharf. *Author's Collection*

This turn of the century view of Newhaven Harbour shows several company vessels tied up at the Railway Wharf, while further down on East Quay sailing barges unload. *Author's Collection*

In the foreground of this Newhaven Harbour view is the swing bridge, this replaced an old drawbridge allowing vessels to reach the North Quay, built in 1891, specifically for the import of Baltic timber. *Author's Collection*

The Customs House viewed from the East Quay. In the background is the London and Paris Hotel. *Author's Collection*

In this general view of Newhaven Harbour we can see four of the Joint Company's passenger ferries as well as the tug *Hauler* tied up to a sailing ship.   *Author's Collection*

Steamers abound in this 1901 view of Newhaven Harbour. The tiny steam vessel seen between the paddler on the left and the tramp steamer *Neptun* is the launch *Imp*, she was used as the harbour runabout and message carrier.   *Author's Collection*

The Signal Station, Newhaven Harbour. *Author's Collection*

Newhaven Harbour. *Author's Collection*

The TrSS *Brighton* of 1901 was the first steam turbine vessel purchased by the LBSCR. It was built by Denny's of Dumbarton and its Parsons' triple expansion turbine engines produced 6,000 hp giving the vessel a top speed of over 21 knots.   *Author's Collection*

In 1905 a second steam turbine vessel joined the fleet, she was the TrSS *Dieppe*. Built by Fairfield of Glasgow her dimensions were similar to the *Brighton*, however, her engines produced 6,500 hp which increased the top speed slightly.   *Author's Collection*

Sister to *Newhaven*, the TrSS *Rouen* was launched in 1912. Commandeered by the French Navy in 1914 she served as an auxiliary cruiser. *Rouen* was torpedoed off Brittany and three crew members were killed but she stayed afloat and was towed to Cherbourg for repairs.
Author's Collection

TrSS *Paris*, launched in 1913, had a top speed of 25 knots which enabled her to complete the channel crossing in only 2¾ hours. *Author's Collection*

Newhaven Harbour, *c.* 1910, a double-ended Isle of Wight ferry is tied up to the quayside. The massive sheerlegs were used to lift boilers and engines out of vessels for repair in the LBSCR's marine workshops seen behind.   *Author's Collection*

The Avant Port, Dieppe. This harbour basin housed the ferry terminus. The four vessels tied up on Quai Henri IV are, left to right: *Sussex*, *Paris*, *Cherbourg* and *Brest*. In the foreground is an early French submarine making its way to the harbour mouth.   *Author's Collection*

cargo route proved to be unsuccessful and so was closed in 1912. The LBSCR vessels *Brittany* (II) and *Normandy* (II) were therefore surplus to requirements and were sold, as was the old paddle steamer *Paris* (II). An unusual crew member on one of the French vessels at this time was one Ho Chi Min, who may have only been a pantry boy but he was destined for higher things.

Early in the morning of 16th March, 1912, *Sussex* was on its way to Newhaven from France and came upon the wreck of the P&O liner *Oceana*. *En route* to Bombay she had been in collision with the sailing vessel *Pisagua*; the latter was only slightly damaged but the *Oceana* was in danger of sinking. *Sussex* lowered her lifeboats and picked up most of the survivors and took them to Newhaven. The tug *Alert* and a merchantman took *Oceana* in tow but she sank before she could be beached, 17 lives were lost. The following year all vessels in the fleet were fitted with wireless telegraphs and were able to converse with shore stations at Newhaven, Dieppe, Boulogne, Niton on the Isle of Wight and any other ships so fitted.

The passenger vessels *Manche* and *Tamise* and the cargo ship *Caen* were sold in 1913, and a new passenger ship the TrSS *Paris* (III) joined the fleet. Delivered to Newhaven in January 1913, *Paris* was built by Denny's of Dumbarton. Fitted with compound single-reduction geared turbines and twin screws the machinery produced 3,500 hp, which in turn produced a top speed of 25 knots. She managed an average crossing time of only 2¾ hours, thereby reducing the London-Paris journey time. This was further reduced from 25th June by the opening of the direct route between Dieppe and Paris (via Pontoise) by the Etat. With the increase in ship speed and the shorter land distance the daylight journey was reduced to eight hours, one hour less than the previous best. A further coal lighter was purchased in 1914, this was numbered SR14 after 1923.

On 4th August, 1914 war was declared between Britain and Germany. The joint fleet, along with those of the SECR, LSWR, GWR and other railway companies were requisitioned by the Government. The French registered vessels were taken over by the French Navy. On 12th August Newhaven was closed to civilian traffic and *Sussex*, the only passenger vessel still working the Newhaven-Dieppe route, was based in Dieppe and ran thrice weekly to Folkestone. *Brest, Cherbourg, Portsmouth, Maine* and *Bordeaux*, with others, assisted in landing the BEF in France. *Paris* and *Anjou* were converted to minesweepers; *Rouen* became an auxiliary warship; *Newhaven, Dieppe* and *Brighton* were converted to hospital ships. On 9th November King George V sailed to France on *Brighton* to visit the troops at the front. On 14th January, 1915 *Paris* became the first LBSCR vessel to be commissioned as a Royal Navy ship, becoming HMS *Paris*. *Arundel* transferred to Dover as a troop transport, and *Portsmouth* was stationed at Deptford for runs to the French coast.

The first war casualty for the joint fleet came on 24th March, 1916 when *Sussex* carrying civilian passengers, was crossing from Folkestone to Dieppe and was torpedoed by a German submarine. The torpedo struck the bows of the ship and blew off most of her forepart, which sank: 74 passengers were killed, mostly American and Spanish, including the composer Enrique Granados. Six crew were also lost. *Sussex* stayed afloat despite her serious damage and was beached on the French coast. Following this incident Dieppe was closed to civilian traffic.

The last passenger vessel purchased by the LBSCR-ETAT partnership was the TrSS *Versailles*. Ordered in 1919 shortages of material after the war meant that she did not join the fleet until 1921.   *Author's Collection*

This Edwardian aerial view of Dieppe Harbour shows an LBSCR passenger ferry heading for the open sea and home. Tied up at the quay are the *Tamise* and three French owned Newhaven-Dieppe cargo vessels.   *Author's Collection*

Rouen became the second joint fleet vessel to feel the wrath of the Hun, being torpedoed off the coast of Brittany. Three crewmen were killed, but again the vessel stayed afloat and she was towed to Cherbourg for repairs. Newhaven was by this stage of the war a hive of activity; on an average day 26 vessels carrying a total of 15,000 men tested the port and railway staff to the limit.

The joint fleet's first total loss came on 17th June, 1917 when *Anjou*, whilst serving as a mine sweeper in the French Navy, struck a mine off Bayonne and sank. She went down in only two minutes and took two Dieppe men with her. *Cherbourg* shared a similar fate later on in the year when she struck a mine and was damaged beyond repair. Another total loss occurred on 21st November when the transport vessel *Maine* was torpedoed *en route* from Newhaven to Dieppe. Twenty-nine crew members perished, including the cabin boy Robert Dinet who was only 14 years old. He was posthumously awarded the Croix de Guerre and the Médaille Militaire by the French Government for his bravery. Fortunately no further joint fleet vessels were lost or damaged during the remainder of the war.

Newhaven hummed with activity during the war years, a new power station, signal box, warehouses and extra sidings being built to handle the extra traffic. Some 19,750 special goods trains, consisting of 866,021 loaded wagons, almost half of which contained ammunition, came to the wharves for onward shipment to France. A total of 6,018,465 tons of ordnance stores, 2,682,756 tons of ammunition and 3,335,709 tons of general stores passed through the port *en route* to France.

At the war's end much work had to be put in to refitting the fleet to passenger work, also thousands of tons of stores and hundreds of thousands of troops were returning from the war zones and passing through Newhaven. The LBSCR purchased two new non-revenue earning vessels in 1919, the MV *Imp*, a small 26 ft launch purchased second-hand, and the lighter MV *Soton*. Slowly the harbour returned to commercial use, and on 5th March, 1919 the port was handed back to the civilian Harbour Board and in July the Newhaven-Dieppe ferry service resumed with a thrice-weekly return trip. A new passenger ferry was ordered in 1919 by the Etat from Forges et Chantiers, to be named the TrSS *Versailles*. She was designed with single reduction steam turbines and an estimated top speed of 25 knots. Shortages of materials following the war meant that she was not launched until 1921. Another new vessel joined the fleet in 1921, the tug SS *Richmere* built by George Brown and Co. of Greenock in 1915.

In 1922 TSS *France* was sold and the last vessel to be purchased by the LBSCR joined the fleet at Newhaven. The tug MV *Foremost 22* was constructed by J. Meyers and Co. of Zaltbommel in Holland. She was fitted out with the most modern equipment and, as well as her towing duties, she could be called upon as a fire fighting and salvage ship. The last Brighton vessel to join the fleet, it is not surprising to find that she was also the last LBSCR ship in service not being sold until 1960.

The following vessels, either jointly or fully owned by the LBSCR, were handed over to the Southern Railway on grouping in 1923: passenger ferries TSS *Arundel*, TrSS *Brighton*, TrSS *Dieppe*, TrSS *Newhaven*, TrSS *Rouen*, TSS *Paris* and TrSS *Versailles*. Cargo ships TSS *Brest*, TSS *Portsmouth* and TSS *Bordeaux*. Non-revenue earning vessels MV *Imp*, MV *Soton*, SS *Richmere*, MV *Foremost 22* and seven coal lighters.

Victorian engraving of Ryde Pier.   *Author's Collection*

The PS *Duchess of Fife* pulls away from the Clarence Pier jetty in Southsea after picking up foot passengers. The ferries would call here ten minutes after leaving the Harbour station to pick up day trippers for the Isle of Wight.   *Author's Collection*

Chapter Three

Portsmouth-Ryde (IOW)

By an Act of Parliament (9 & 10 Vict. cap. 107 of July 1846) the Portsmouth Harbour Pier Company was authorised to build a pier from the Common Hard at the Eastern or Portsmouth side of the Portsmouth Harbour, for vessels between Portsmouth and the Isle of Wight at Ryde, where a pier had first been built as far back as 1814. The Portsmouth and Ryde Steam Packet Company (P&RSPC) was the main user of the new pier with its vessels PS *Union*, PS *Lord Yarborough*, PS *Earl Spencer*, PS *Prince Albert* and PS *Her Majesty*. A second company began using the facilities in 1850, this being the Portsea, Portsmouth, Gosport and Isle of Wight New Steam Packet Company. The New Steam Packet Co. had two vessels, the PS *Prince Of Wales* and the PS *Princess Royal*, and ran in competition for only one year before being taken over by the P&RSPC, which in the meantime had changed its name to the Portsmouth and Ryde Joint Stock Steam Packet Co. Following the takeover the company name changed yet again to the Port of Portsmouth and Ryde United Steam Packet Company; short company names were obviously not in vogue at this time.

On the Isle of Wight railway construction had begun with a line from Newport to Cowes, and continued with the Isle of Wight Railway opening its line from Ryde to Shanklin on 23rd August, 1864, and continuing on to Ventnor by September 1866. The rail-ferry-rail link was now almost complete, with the Portsmouth station (opened in 1847 jointly by the LBSCR and the LSWR) being about mile from the ferry terminal at the Southsea Pier.

In 1865 a tramway was built by a private company from the Portsmouth Town station to the pierhead at Southsea Pier, providing the final link in the transport chain. This was an improvement on the previous situation, but it still involved passengers changing from railway carriage to horse-drawn tram or vice versa. A traveller who made the journey in 1872 wrote this of his experience: 'The scramble at Portsmouth for tram accommodation was not an agreeable experience and with a party of children, nurses with luggage, perambulators and bath tubs, a man had to be something of an organiser to get through without losing his temper and some of his belongings as well'. The joint railway companies were not happy with this situation and pushed ahead with plans for their own line to the sea.

It must be mentioned here that the reason the original Portsmouth station was not closer to the Naval Dockyard was the fact that the important docks were ringed with a defensive line of walls and forts which the Navy would not allow to be breached at that time. By the 1870s the international situation had settled into a long period of peace, also a new ring of forts had been built up on the hills above Portsmouth with massive long range guns. The way was now open for the old inner defences to be opened up for roads and railways.

After negotiations with the Admiralty the LBSCR and the LSWR reached an agreement that allowed the building of a railway from the Portsmouth Town station to the harbour. Known as the Joint Line, authorisation was given under the Joint Portsmouth Railway Extension Act, 36 & 37 Vict. cap. 68 of 7th July,

Clarence Pier.   *Reproduced from the 25", 1896 Ordnance Survey Map*

1873 to build two railway lines. The first was from Portsmouth Town station to a terminus built on a new pier in Portsmouth Harbour, and the second was an extension of the first from a junction just short of the terminus to Watering Island by means of a steel bridge across a corner of the harbour. At the insistence of the Admiralty a siding came off the pier line to the Old Gun Wharf. This final part of the line was the price paid to their Lords of the Admiralty for the breaching of the fortifications. The Portsmouth Harbour station opened to passenger traffic on 2nd October, 1876.

Meanwhile across the Solent on the Isle of Wight the Ryde Pier Company, encouraged by the arrival of the IOW Railway at St Johns Road in Ryde, had first built a tramway down the length of the pier (built in 1864) and then this was extended to the St Johns Rd terminus in August 1871. The tramway was standard gauge and horse drawn. In 1875 a line was opened from Ryde to Newport by the IOW Central Railway. The extra traffic generated by the new line caused such an overload that the tramway was unable to cope and the joint companies felt the need to act. They decided to build a new pier at Ryde, long enough so as to not be affected by the tides, and at the same time build a railway from the pierhead to the St Johns Rd terminus of the IOW Railway. Despite desperate action by the tram company to retain its passenger monopoly it was overwhelmed by the might of the joint railway companies. An Act, entitled the South Western and Brighton Railway Companies (Isle of Wight and Ryde Pier Railway), was passed under 40 & 41 Vict. cap. 107 of 23rd July, 1877. This enabled the joint companies to build a new pier at Ryde immediately to the east of the old pier and construct a line of railway which followed the line of the tramway, with the exception of a short length which cut off a sharp bend by means of a tunnel under the Strand Road. A new station was built at the landward end of the pier and called Esplanade. The line from St Johns Road to Esplanade station was opened on 5th April, 1880, the line from Esplanade station to the pierhead being opened to passenger traffic on 12th July, 1880.

The joint companies had not remained content with owning the piers and railways at each end of this route, they also moved to fill in the gap between. By Act of Parliament, the South Western and Brighton Railway Companies (Steam vessels) Act of 1879, 42 & 43 Vict. cap. 30 dated 30th May, the companies were empowered to 'provide and use steam and other vessels for conveyance of traffic between places on the coast of Hampshire and between places on the Isle of Wight'. To accomplish this the LSWR and the LBSCR formed a new company known as the South Western and Brighton Railway Companies Steam Packet Service, or the Joint Company for short. The vessels for this fleet were acquired by buying out the Port of Portsmouth and Ryde United Steam Packet Company, at a cost of £38,000. The ships concerned were the PS *Albert Edward* built by Oswald Mordant of Southampton in 1878, PS *Alexandra* built in 1879 by Scott & Co., PS *Duke of Edinburgh* from the Money, Wigram shipyard in 1869, PS *Heather Bell* from Blackwood and Gordon in 1876, PS *Prince Consort* an old vessel built in 1859 by J. Scott Russel of London, PS *Princess Alice* another Money, Wigram vessel dating from 1869 and the PS *Princess of Wales* built by Lewis & Stockwell in 1865. In addition to these passenger vessels two coal hulks, the *Dragon* and the *Enterprise* and two tow boats were included in the deal.

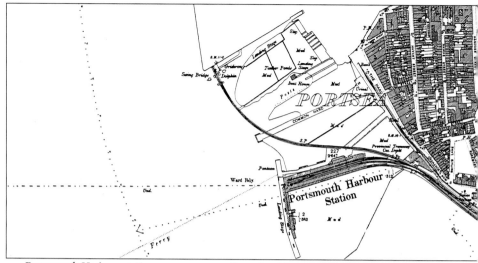

Portsmouth Harbour station.   *Reproduced from the 25", 1896 Ordnance Suvey Map*

Ryde Pier and Espalande.   *Reproduced from the 6", 1862 Ordnance Suvey Map*

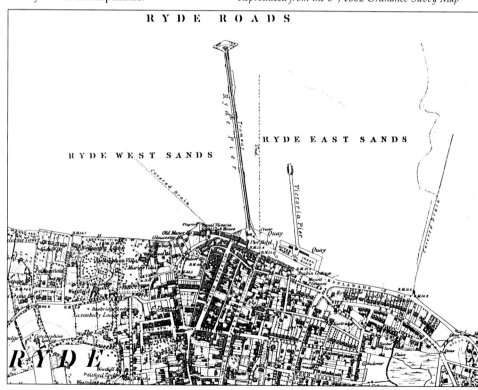

Receipts from the route were split ⅔ to the South Western and ⅓ to the Brighton. This was because the LSWR was the major shareholder in the deal and also in recognition of the fact that more revenue would be generated from its shorter route to London.

On 2nd November, 1881 a new vessel, the PS *Victoria*, built by Aitken and Mansel at their yard at Whiteinch, was added to the fleet list. *Victoria* was unusual in being the first double-ended vessel on the cross-Solent route. Cut in half amidships one end would be the mirror of the other. This strange layout was to enable the craft to enter and leave berths without the bother, and danger, of turning. She cost £17,000 to build and was 191 ft long, 45½ ft across the beam and could carry 700 passengers in unheard of comfort. In 1882 two of the older ships, the PS *Prince Consort* and the PS *Princess Alice* were sent to the breaker's yard. In 1884 the PS *Duchess of Connaught* and PS *Duchess of Edinburgh* joined the fleet; built to the same design and virtually identical they came from the Glasgow yard of Aitken & Mansel at a cost of £36,800. These too were double-ended vessels but of an interior standard even higher than *Victoria*. Two more of the old United ships were disposed of in 1884 and 1885, they were the PS *Duke of Edinburgh* and the PS *Princess of Wales*.

A further two new vessels were purchased in 1889 and 1893; four years apart but once again to the same design they were the PS *Duchess of Albany* and the PS *Margaret*, the latter replacing the PS *Albert Edward* which had been sold. Under the articles of agreement signed by the builders, Scott & Co. of Greenock (who also built the PS *Duchess of Albany*), and the joint company the *Princess* was to be fitted with 'a complete pair of surface condensing diagonal engines with an athwartships condenser and one double-ended boiler'. Clause 2 of the agreement gave a required delivery date of 1st June, 1893. Clause 4 gave the purchase price of the vessel as £10,000, to be paid in four equal parts, one to be paid when the frame was laid, the second when the hull had been plated, the third when the ship had been launched and the last once the vessel had been delivered and had passed her sea trials. Clause 5 commented on the speed requirement on the sea trials, 14 knots at 100 lb. of steam pressure. Failure to reach the required speed would be penalised by the company withholding £50 for every tenth of a knot less than 14 from the final payment. The general description of the vessel included the following:

... to have a saloon sunk into the upper-deck abaft the engines with a large promenade deck for passengers, dining saloon forward under deck. Cabins, to have a raised saloon aft with plate glass windows and neatly finished in yellow pine. At aft end to have a ladies' saloon with WC. The saloon to be supplied with a mahogany or teak table, a neat stove with a brass funnel and suitable lamps. Floor to be covered in Brussels carpet. The cushions to be stuffed with best horse hair and covered in crimson plush velvet.

Certificated for 400 passengers each, these two vessels were the last double-ended ships to be purchased for this route as this experiment had proved to be a failure.

In 1897 the PS *Duchess of Kent* was purchased, she was built by Day, Summers & Co. for excursion duties and could carry up to 870 passengers. Two years

Portsmouth Harbour station, opened in October 1876 as the LBSCR's mainland link with the Isle of Wight. Tied up at the pier is the PS *Princess Margaret* which was launched in 1893 as a replacement for the old PS *Albert Edward*. The PS *Princess Margaret* was sold in 1927.

Author's Collection

An Edwardian view of the Portsmouth Harbour station, in the background can be seen the pier siding going off to the Gun Wharf. This was built as part of the price required by the Lords of the Admiralty for breaching the Portsmouth land defences.   *Author's Collection*

Ryde Pier, Isle of Wight, in the foreground is the Esplanade station opened in April 1880.
Author's Collection

Ryde Pier, *c.* 1890, looking towards the town. On the left is the horse-drawn tram used to carry foot passengers who did not wish to walk the length of the pier to the town. In the centre is the Joint company's standard gauge track, and on the right is the promenade.   *L. Marshall*

65   RYDE (Isle of Wight). — Ryde from the Pier. — LL.

This Edwardian view of Ryde Pier shows the Life Boat station which was built on the side of the pier at the turn of the century.   *Author's Collection*

The PS *Duchess of Fife* ties up to the Ryde Pier loaded with another boat load of day trippers for the Isle of Wight.   *Author's Collection*

The PS *Duchess of Edinburgh*, a double-ended vessel built in 1884 by Aitken & Maunsel. The purchase price of £36,800 must have been repaid many times over before she was sold out of service in 1910. *Author's Collection*

An unfortunately overexposed photograph of the PS *Princess Margaret* on her way to Portsmouth Harbour. Built in 1893 by Scott & Co. of Greenock at a cost of £10,000 she had a top speed of 14 knots at 100 1b. of steam pressure. *Author's Collection*

Launched in 1897 the PS *Duchess of Kent* was licensed to carry 870 passengers on the cross-Solent route.   *Author's Collection*

The PS *Duchess of Kent* beached on the Southsea foreshore after a collision with the collier *Transporter* on 3rd September, 1909. All 400 passengers were safely taken off and two days later she was refloated and made her own way to Southampton for repairs.   *Author's Collection*

later the PS *Duchess of Fife* was launched from the Clydebank Engineering and Shipbuilding yard, fitted with double crank, simple engines working at 150 lb. pressure to produce 15½ knots at 600 rpm. Again built for excursions round the Isle of Wight and along the South Coast, her large size and general seaworthiness meant she could venture out in weather which kept most of her rivals in port. It was said that if her Captain, Charles Gubbey, had his long beard tucked inside his jacket then the trip was going to be a rough one.

The last of the old Ryde United passenger ships, *Heather Bell*, was disposed of in 1899 as was the PS *Victoria,* the first joint vessel. In mid-August 1903 the *Duchess of Albany* collided with the yacht *Wintonia* at the entrance to Portsmouth Harbour. The skipper of the *Duchess* was found to be at fault, but only because his forward view was impeded by the crowds of passengers on deck at the time. From then on all new ships were constructed with an exclusive forward view bridge for the use of the ship's officers and all the older vessels were modified. After the changes in 1899 the fleet list remained unchanged for eight years, but then in 1908 the PS *Duchess of Edinburgh* was sold.

Another collision occurred in Portsmouth Harbour on 3rd September, 1909 when the PS *Duchess of Kent* collided with the collier *Transporter*. The *Kent* immediately began to take on water and was quickly beached on the shore near to the Victoria Pier. Her 400 passengers were safely taken off before she sank. Two days later she was patched up and refloated, then she made her own way to Southampton for repairs. The PS *Princess Margaret* was also unlucky when entering Portsmouth Harbour in March 1910. Whilst turning in the harbour a heavy swell carried her on to the moored destroyer HMS *Crane*. Although she was holed and had a lifeboat ripped off she managed to carry on to her berth at the pier and unload her passengers; later she sailed to Newhaven for repairs.

In 1910 and 1911 two new sister ships joined the fleet, they were the PS *Duchess of Richmond* and the PS *Duchess of Norfolk* both built by D. & W. Henderson of Glasgow. *Richmond* replaced the PS *Duchess of Connaught* which was withdrawn and sold. The last alteration to the fleet list prior to World War I was the sale of the PS *Alexandra* in 1913.

At the outbreak of war in 1914 several of the passenger vessels were commandeered for naval use. The PS *Duchess of Fife*, PS *Duchess of Kent*, PS *Duchess of Richmond* and PS *Duchess of Norfolk* all served as minesweepers. Only the PS *Duchess of Albany* and the PS *Princess Margaret* remained in service on the Portsmouth-Ryde route. The PS *Duchess of Richmond* was mined and sunk whilst on minesweeping duties in the Mediterranean in 1915, but fortunately all the other vessels survived the war to return to peacetime duties in 1919.

At the 1923 Grouping five passenger vessels were handed over to the Southern Railway, the Duchesses of *Albany, Fife, Kent* and *Norfolk* and the PS *Princess Margaret*. As well as the passenger ships the joint companies owned a total of five horse boats, three more having been purchased, of which numbers 1, 4 and 5 were still in service. Also on the fleet list were two launches, both named *Ada*, the second of which was launched in 1910 and made it to the Grouping. To pull the horse boats the company had built a powerful tug, the *Adur II*, in 1912, this vessel lasted until 1925 in Southern Railway ownership before being sold. The horse boats, or tow boats, were at first for the

Built in 1899 for excursion traffic the PS *Duchess of Fife* was commandeered by the Royal Navy in 1914 for mine sweeping duties. Returned to her owners in 1919 she continued in service until sold by the Southern Railway in 1929.   *Author's Collection*

The last vessel built for the LBSCR/LSWR Joint Co. was the PS *Duchess of Norfolk*. Launched in 1911 she was one of several railway ships to serve as mine sweepers during World War I.
                                                                                                            Author's Collection

South Western & Brighton Railway Companies' Steam Packet Service
—— TO AND FROM THE ——

ISLE OF WIGHT

OCTOBER 1922, and until further notice
(Weather and other circumstances permitting).

S.S. " Duchess of Fife," " Duchess of Kent," " Duchess of Norfolk," " Duchess of Albany " and " Princess Margaret."

PORTSMOUTH HARBOUR AND SOUTHSEA CLARENCE PIER TO RYDE

		a.m.	a.m.	a.m.	a.m.	a.m.	a.m.	p.m.	p.m.	p.m.	p.m.	p.m.	p.m.	p.m.		p.m.		a.m.	p.m.	p.m.	p.m.	p.m.
Portsmouth Harbour	dep.	2.40	.7.5	7.35	9.25	10.0	11.40	12.15	1.50	3.15	3.55	4.50	6.10	7.15		11.30		10.15	12.20	2.10	4.0	6.55
Southsea Clarence Pier	,,	..	..	..	..	10.10	11.50	..	2.0	..	4.5	5.0	..	7.25	*Thursdays only*		*October only*	10.25	12.30	2.20	4.10	7.5
Ryde Pier	.. arr.	3.10	7.35	8.5	9.55	10.35	12.15	12.45	2.25	3.45	4.30	5.25	6.40	7.50		12.0		10.50	12.55	2.45	4.35	7.30

RYDE TO SOUTHSEA CLARENCE PIER AND PORTSMOUTH HARBOUR

		a.m.	a.m.	a.m.	a.m.	a.m.	a.m.	p.m.	p.m.	p.m.	p.m.	p.m.	p.m.	p.m.		Midt.		a.m.	p.m.	p.m.	p.m.	p.m.
Ryde Pier	dep.	6.45	7.55	8.40	10.10	11.10	12.55	2.20	3.5	4.0	4.50	5.45	6.50	9.25	*Thursdays only*	12.5	*October only*	11.10	1.10	3.10	5.0	9.25
Southsea Clarence Pier	arr.	..	..	..	10.35	11.35	1.20	..	3.30	..	5.15	6.10	..	..				11.35	1.35	3.35	..	..
Portsmouth Harbour	,,	7.15	8.25	9.10	10.45	11.45	1.30	2.50	3.40	4.30	5.25	6.20	7.20	9.55		12.35		11.45	1.45	3.45	5.30	9.55

REVISED FARES :

	Single		Return	
	1st	2nd	1st	2nd
To Ryde Pier Gates, and vice versa. ...	2/2	1/7	4/-	3/2
	(Including all Pier Tolls)			
To Ryde Pier Head, and vice versa. ...	2/-	1/5	3/8	2/10
	(Exclusive of Ryde Pier Tolls)			

For particulars of
CHEAP DAY RETURN TICKETS
between Portsmouth Harbour, Southsea
Clarence Pier and Ryde
SEE SEPARATE ANNOUNCEMENTS

ORDINARY RETURN TICKETS ARE AVAILABLE FOR TWO DAYS (Including day of issue and return).

Those issued on Saturday are available to return on the following Monday. Children between three and twelve are charged half-fares.

The connection between the Trains and Boats and vice versa is not guaranteed, neither will the Joint Companies be accountable for any loss, inconvenience, or injury arising from sea risks or delays.

Passengers are requested to look to their luggage on entering and leaving the Steam Packets, and before embarking to see it labelled to the Station or Pier where the journey of the owner terminates. Passengers are allowed to take with them, free of charge, the following amounts of personal luggage : 1st Class 150 lbs., 3rd Class 100 lbs. Excess Luggage will be charged for at the rates applicable.

Goods or Merchandise not allowed as passengers' luggage, and will be charged for at Parcels Tariff.

SEASON TICKET RATES :–First Class. Twelve Months, £3 : os. od. Six Months, £5 : os. od. Three Months, £3 : os. od. Two Months £2 : 9s. 6d. One Month. £1 : 10s. od. Available for all advertised passages between Ryde, and the Piers at Portsmouth, exclusive of Pier Tolls.

Season Tickets, exclusive of Pier Tolls, are issued at half rates for residential purposes only, to all applicants under 16 years of age, and to Scholars, Students, Apprentices, Articled Clerks and Articled Pupils (in receipt of salary, wages, or any monetary allowance whatsoever, not exceeding 18/- per week), up to 18 years of age.

Quarterly Tickets may be extended to six or twelve months on payment of the difference between the periodical rates, but tickets must be promptly renewed or the privilege will be forfeited. Application for Season Tickets should be made at the Marine Superintendent's Office, Portsmouth Harbour Pier.

CONVEYANCE OF MOTOR VEHICLES (Which can be run on and off Boats with own power), Horses, Carriages, Vans, Cattle, etc., TO & FROM THE ISLE OF WIGHT on Week Days, by powerful Steam Tug and Tow Boats.
(Weather and other circumstances permitting)

From PORTSMOUTH (Broad St. Slipway) for RYDE
About TWO HOURS before High Water.

From RYDE (George St. Slipway) for PORTSMOUTH
About HALF-AN-HOUR before High Water.

Information as to actual times of departure from Portsmouth and Ryde may be obtained at the Marine Superintendent's Offices, Broad Street, Portsmouth (Tel. 4655), Portsmouth Harbour Pier (Tel. 6077), or from the Station Master, Ryde (Tel. 247).

Senders or Owners of Horses, Carriages, Motor Cars. Live Stock, etc., by Tow Boat, take upon themselves all risk of Conveyance, and of loading or unloading, as the Companies will not be answerable for accidents or damage done to any property, live stock, etc. All traffic must be at the place of embarkation half-an-hour before time of sailing, and in charge of Senders' or Owners' Servants who must accompany it.

RATES (at Owner's Risk)

		£ s. d.			£ s. d.			£ s. d.
Motor Cars	not exceeding		Van, not exceeding 15ft. in length			Cattle, if over 10 in number .. each	4	0
See Note (A)	10 cwt., Single Journey	1 1 0	(Loaded) £3 0 0 Empty	1 4 0	When only 1 Horse or Bullock		
	10 cwt., Return ,, (B)	1 16 0	,, not exceeding 18ft. in length		in the Boat	10	0
	above		(Loaded) £4 0 0 .. ,,	1 10 0	Yearlings .. .. .. each	3	0
	10 cwt., Single ..	1 11 0	Farm Waggon (Loaded) £2 0 0 ,,	16 0	Sheep, Lambs and Pigs—		
	10 cwt., Return ,, (B)	2 16 0	Four-wheel Carriage	1 12 0	under half-a-score .. each	1	0
Motor Tricar	..	10 0	,, ,, (Loaded)	2 2 0	over half-a-score up to 1 score	9	0
Motor Bicycle	..	3 0	Light 4-wheel Carriage, drawn by		above a single score per score	7	0
,, ,, with Side Car	..	6 0	Ponies or 1 Horse	1 0 0	Calves .. .. .. each	2	6
Bicycle	..	1 0	Gig, Cart or other 2-wheel Vehicle	16 0	Servants, in charge, who must		
Hand Truck or Barrow	..	1 6	Horse with Carriage	5 0	accompany all Horses, etc. each	1	0
Hand Organ	..	2 8	,, not with Carriage	7 0	Dogs .. .. .. each		8
Van, not exceeding 12ft. in length			Cattle, if under 10 in number .. each	6 9	Hearse with Corpse	2	2 0
(Loaded) £2 8 0 Empty	1 0 0							

(A) Including Portsmouth Corporation Dues.   (B) Return Tickets are available for one month.
Motor Lorries, Steam Traction Engines, Circuses, etc., Quotations by special arrangements with Marine Superintendent.

BY ORDER.

LBSCR/LSWR Joint ferry timetable for October 1922.   *Author's Collection*

conveyance of live stock and carriages and later for motor cars. They operated between the slipway at Broad Street, Portsmouth, and the slipway at Georges Street, Ryde.

As a postscript to this joint steamer venture it must be added that the LSWR had purchased on its own account the Stokes Bay Railway and Pier Company (SBR&PC) in 1875. The railway branching out of Gosport station, ran down to a new pier constructed by the SBR&PC and opened in 1863. The LSWR ran the line from the outset, but the ferries were run by the Isle of Wight Ferry Company with three ships, the PS *Victoria*, PS *Chancellor* and PS *Garloch*. In 1872 the entire enterprise, line, pier and ferries was leased to the South Western for 999 years, but in 1875, as previously stated, the whole issue was purchased by the LSWR. Although owned by the South Western the receipts were still split in the same manner as for the Portsmouth-Ryde route. From the early 1890s the joint vessels PS *Duchess of Albany* and the PS *Princess Margaret* worked the route. The Stokes Bay service was discontinued in 1913 and the branch line and pier sold to the Admiralty in 1922.

The Solent, Portsmouth, Stokes Bay and Ryde.

Chapter Four

Littlehampton-Channel Islands and France

The LBSCR opened its West Coast Line from Brighton to Chichester in 1846. The station named Littlehampton was in fact at Lyminster, 1½ miles north of the town. Shortly after leaving Littlehampton station the line crossed the River Arun, the bridge used being of a singularly unusual design which involved one section of the bridge sliding back into the other in a telescopic action. The bridge was built for a single track only and increases in the traffic meant that by the late 1850s the bridge was becoming a major bottleneck. The railway company sought to improve the flow of trains by seeking permission to upgrade the bridge to a fixed span, with double track. The Littlehampton Harbour and River Commissioners, who were responsible for the Arun from Littlehampton to Arundel, came down against the plan and pledged to fight its construction as the design for the bridge showed a reduction of the navigable channel from 60 to 40 feet. As part of the deal which was finally thrashed out with the commissioners the LBSCR agreed to build a railway line from Pulborough to Littlehampton, via Arundel. The Littlehampton branch was to have a wharf on the harbour with sidings and a railway connection to the branch line.

The Mid Sussex Junction Railway, of which the Littlehampton branch was part, received its Royal Assent under 23 & 24 Vict., cap. 171 on 23rd July, 1860. The Act also authorised the purchase of 1,000 yards of river frontage at Littlehampton on which to build a wharf. The original, perhaps over-optimistic, estimate for the opening date for the new line was May or June of 1863, these months passed and the line was still unfinished. The *West Sussex Gazette* of 18th June gives a good reason for the late completion of the works: 'In their construction, in connection with earthworks, at least 25,000 cubic feet of timber will be consumed, and the quantity of iron is almost fabulous. Over much of the length of frontage there has been great difficulty in driving the piles, the soil being a clayey conglomerate, with stones and shells'. Work was finally completed two months behind schedule and the line and wharf opened to traffic on 17th August, 1863.

Once opened the new wharf was used at first by small coastal vessels, but it was not long before local entrepreneurs saw the chance to make money. On 12th November, 1863 a steam packet service was started between Littlehampton and the Channel Islands. Once again our ever present reporter from the *West Sussex Gazette* had something to say on the matter:

> . . . a continental steam packet service was inaugurated by the arrival of the first cargo boat, the *Vibourg*, from Jersey and St Malo, on Wednesday of last week, with a cargo of wine, brandy, eggs, fruit, etc. By great despatch, the cargo was discharged in time for the *Vibourg* to sail on her return voyage in the evening, and on the Saturday at three o'clock in the afternoon, the first passenger and cargo boat (*Rouen*) sailed for St Malo and Guernsey.

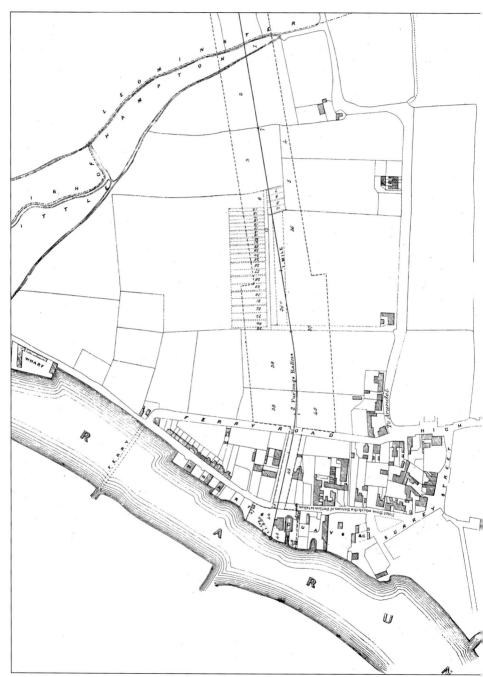

Littlehampton Branch Railway, 1845.

An engraving of the telescopic bridge over the River Arun at Ford. Built in 1845 it had become a white elephant by the 1860s. In order to replace it with a twin-track fixed bridge the Arun River Commissioners made the LBSCR build a railway line from Arundel to Littlehampton.

Author's Collection

Littlehampton Branch Railway, 1858/1859.

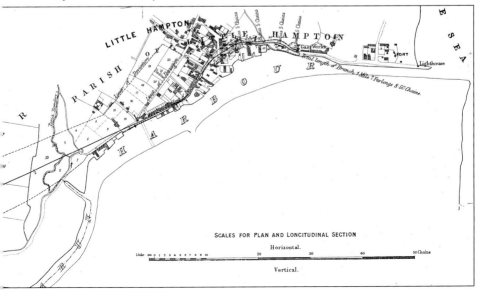

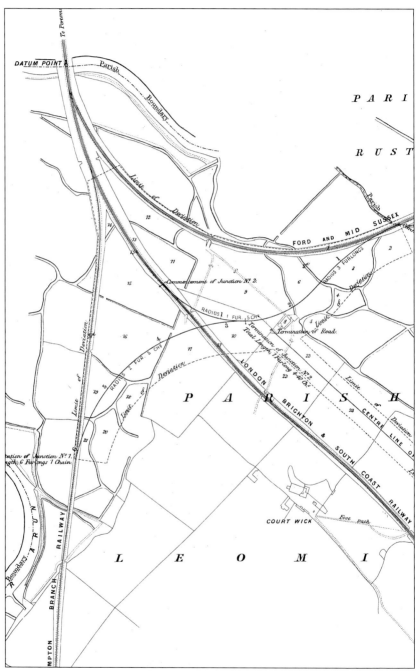

Littlehampton Branch Railway, 1866.

These vessels were owned by the same Mr Maples who had just recently failed as a shipping magnate supplying vessels for the Newhaven-Dieppe route for the LBSCR.

In February 1864 the Littlehampton, Havre and Honfleur Steam Ship Company reached an agreement with the LBSCR whereby they had the use of the facilities at the Littlehampton railway wharf. The railway company sought to improve the trade going through the port and applied for powers to run passenger steamer services to France and the Channel Islands. These powers were granted on 30th June, 1864 under the title of the South Coast Railway Company (Steamboats) Act, 27 & 28 Vict. cap. 154. The Act recites that

. . . by means of the Railways belonging to the London, Brighton and South Coast Railway Company a continuous and direct Line of Communication from the Metropolis and from many other Towns is afforded to Littlehampton in the County of Sussex, which is a convenient Place for the shipping or landing of Passengers and other Traffic to or from various Places on the Coast of France and in the Channel Islands; that it would be of public advantage if the Company were empowered to establish and use Steam Vessels to run between Littlehampton and the several places on the Coast of France and in the Channel Islands which are specified in the Schedule to this Act annexed, and it is expedient that the Company should be authorised to establish and use Steam Vessels, and Powers to raise Money for such Purposes by the Creation of Shares or Stock in their Undertakings, and by Borrowing.

Clause 2 continues:

The Company from Time to Time may build, purchase or hire, and may use, maintain, and work Steam Vessels for the Purpose of carrying on a convenient and efficient Communication by means thereof between Littlehampton and the several Places on the Coast of France and in the Channel Islands specified in the Schedule to this Act annexed.

Clause 4 gives the rates for fares to be charged on the routes from Littlehampton, these were 1st class 3*d*. per mile, 2nd class 2*d*. per mile and 3rd class 1¼*d*. per mile. Clause 5 gives the details of the luggage permissible to each class as 120 lb., 100 lb., and 60 lb. respectively.

The schedule annexed to the Act gave the names of the ports to which the services would be run, and their distances from Littlehampton as follows:

Names	*Computed distances in miles from Littlehampton*
Havre	95 miles
Honfleur	100 miles
St Malo	180 miles
Caen	110 miles
St Peters (Guernsey)	125 miles
St Helier (Jersey)	150 miles

The last of the work to complete the facilities at the wharf was completed only a few months before the Act became law and the *Gazette* reporter was moved to comment on the wharf as part of a larger article on a ship launch at Harvey's shipyard. 'The railway wharves are completed, a steam crane is erected for

Littlehampton Harbour.

Reproduced from the 25", 1876 Ordnance Survey Map

unloading vessels, and there are now running to and from Littlehampton steamers for Jersey and Honfleur'.

The LBSCR steamer service began in January 1865 with a twice-weekly service to Honfleur, this was increased to three times a week in January 1866. This was followed from 1st March, 1866 with a twice-weekly service to St Malo, the Channel Islands and the Isle of Wight. The first vessel purchased by the railway company for these new services was the SS *Ida*, followed shortly by the SS *Rennes*. The *Ida*, previously named the *Mortje Flors*, was built in 1858 at Stockton, whilst the *Rennes* was purchased new from the Millwall Iron Works, London, in 1866.

The Isle of Wight service was dropped after only one year following a disastrous summer season. Another blow followed in December 1864 when the Littlehampton, Havre and Honfleur Steam Ship Company withdrew its services from the railway wharf. Records show that in the first full year of use the railway wharf was used by 128 steamers. Further blows struck the new services in January 1865 when the Jersey-St Malo route was closed and again in 1866 when the Channel Island packet was withdrawn. The reason for the closures was that the LSWR had these routes sewn up with their Weymouth and Southampton services. Trading levels fell so low that eventually the railway company had to call it a day, and so on 1st January, 1867 all LBSCR shipping services were transferred to Newhaven. The Littlehampton-Honfleur service was, however, continued by a private firm which chartered the LBSCR's vessels. The transfer of the shipping services to Newhaven caused a dramatic drop in harbour revenues, £800 in 1867 alone.

Traffic did not cease at the port altogether, and in fact after the initial decline it rose steadily, so much so that in 1869 the LBSCR decided that the increase in traffic merited the resumption of full services from Littlehampton. The timetable showed daily each way sailings, less Sunday, to Honfleur throughout the month. First class fares from London to Honfleur were 21s. single and 31s. 6d. return; 2nd class 15s. single and 22s. 6d. return; and 3rd class 12s. single and 18s. return.

In 1872 a third vessel was purchased for the route, this was the cargo ship SS *Viking*. SS *Honfleur* joined the fleet in 1875 and was to be the last vessel purchased for the Littlehampton services.

The main imports through the port were eggs, butter, fruit and vegetables from farms on the Normandy Peninsular, and coal brought down from the north of England by coaster. In the 1870s the average annual import of dairy products was 4,200 tons of eggs and 4,500 tons of butter, as well as large amounts of cheese, poultry and wine.

By 1878 the activities at the company's main port of Newhaven had expanded to such a degree that it was again decided to withdraw the services from Littlehampton and move them down the coast to Newhaven. The railway continued to serve the wharf with its normal facilities, usually handling coal, but also, in 1880, 2,000 tons of sugar.

In 1914, after the outbreak of World war I, the harbour was taken over by the military authorities to dispatch war stores to France and it was closed to civilian traffic. The port's contribution to the war effort was a total of 787,345 tons of

Advertisement for the Littlehampton ferries and cargo vessels for France, November 1869.
Author's Collection

A busy Edwardian view of the Railway Wharf at Littlehampton. Steam and sail are both tied up to the quayside to take on cargoes of coal loaded by the mobile steam crane.
Author's Collection

Painting of Littlehampton Harbour in 1890, by Maurice Randall.   *Author's Collection*

This pre-1914 panoramic view of Littlehampton Harbour shows the Railway Wharf on the extreme left of the picture. The harbour tug, PS *Jumna*, steams towards the camera.

Author's Collection

A hand crane is used to lift a small marine steam boiler on the Railway Wharf at Littlehampton in this 1910 photograph. *Author's Collection*

Edwardian Littlehampton, the *Worthing Belle* backs out of her berth at the start of a pleasure cruise along the Sussex coast. In the foreground is the harbour tug *Jumna*. *Author's Collection*

Harbour and Pleasure Steamers, Littlehampton

stores sent to France loaded on a total of 2,098 transport vessels. On return trips these ships carried wounded soldiers and servicemen going home on leave. Towards the end of the war captured enemy ordnance passed through the port on the way to War Bond Rallies all over the country. Following the cessation of hostilities in 1918 the port was handed back to the civilian authorities and was, by the Grouping in 1923, slowly getting back to pre-war levels of activity.

The *Honfleur*, 1875, built by Gourley Bros of Dundee; she worked the French ports first from Littlehampton and then from Newhaven.   *Author's Collection*

Unloading captured German guns at Littlehampton's railway wharf, 1918.
Author's Collection

Chapter Five

Langston Wharf-St Helens (IOW)

Langston, or Langstone as the locals spell it, is situated on the north-east corner of Langstone Harbour, a natural harbour almost land locked by Hayling Island to the east and Portsea Island to the west; the harbour is just inside the south-eastern borders of Hampshire.

The LBSCR had opened a station at Havant, one mile to the north on the main Brighton to Portsmouth line, in 1847. The first time the Brighton company had any dealings with the wharf was in 1865 when the Hayling Island Railway, a private venture, was opened for goods traffic to Langston Wharf on 19th January, 1865. The line came from a bay platform in Havant station and ran down to Langston Halt where sidings ran off on either side of the track to the wharves. The entire line to Hayling Island was opened to passenger traffic on 27th July, 1867.

The wharves were in the shape of an inverted 'V', the left-hand fork protruding into the harbour for 700 yards, but only the last 300 yards were constructed in such a way to allow vessels to be loaded or unloaded against it. There was a line of sidings beside the wharf which joined the branch line at the start of the pier. The branch line also ran down the pier from which it crossed over the harbour and onto Hayling Island by means of a 1,000 ft trestle bridge. The right-hand pier was only 400 yards long and had a single line of track for most of its length, being doubled for the last 100 yards. This siding joined the branch line 200 yards to the north of the junction with the left pier siding. The public road also shared the right hand pier and crossed the harbour by a second trestle bridge; both bridges had central sections which were able to swing aside to allow the passage of vessels.

The usual traffic through the wharf was wagon loads of building material, lumber, coal and road stone for shipment to the Isle of Wight. On 1st January, 1872 the Hayling Railway was taken over by the LBSCR.

Meanwhile on the other side of the Solent, the Brading Harbour Improvement and Railway Act of 1874 had authorised the building of a railway line from Brading to Bembridge via St Helens Quay. The company behind the Act was the Isle of Wight Marine Transit Company (IOWMT), which had made an agreement with the LBSCR to run a cargo ferry from St Helens Quay, IOW, to Langston Wharf. The Brighton company agreed to the proposal provided that the route did not enter into competition with its own Portsmouth-Ryde service.

The Bembridge-St Helens Quay line was opened on 27th May, 1882 and from its inception was operated by the Isle of Wight Railway, from whose station at Brading the branch line emanated.

To operate the ferry service the IOWMT purchased, through one of its Directors, Mr S.L. Mason, the ex-North British Railway's vessel PS *Carrier*. Built in 1858 for the Tayport to Broughty Ferry service across the River Tay, it stayed in service until 1878 when the Tay Bridge was opened. Following the disastrous

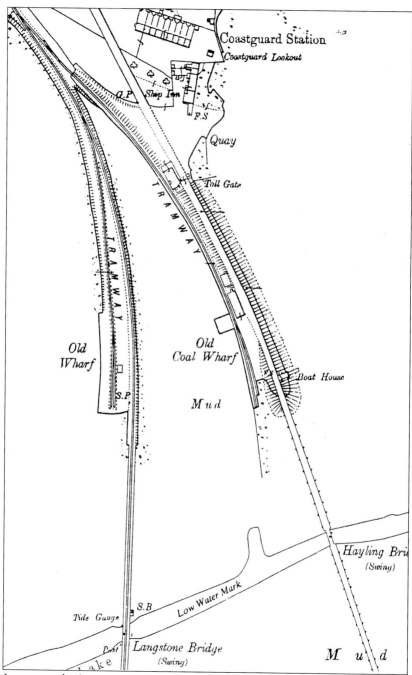

Langstone wharf.

Reproduced from the 25″, 1909 Ordnance Survey Map

collapse of the bridge in 1879, the ferry was reinstated, and *Carrier* continued its Tay crossings until 1882 when it was considered to be too old for further service. Mr Mason, who was also a Director of the NBR, purchased the vessel and its movable cradles and lifting gear for £3,400.

The PS *Carrier* was 124 ft long and 24.7 ft wide, its draught was only 5 ft 9 in. fully loaded. It was fitted with two 60 hp engines which turned a single crank. *Carrier* was flush-decked with two rows of rails laid on it, the rails being laid in such a way that the normal 6 ft way was reduced to only 4 ft 8½ in., therefore allowing the centre set of rails to be used if there was not a full load available. Fourteen wagons could be loaded on board *Carrier* at any one time, the usual layout being seven loaded wagons on one side and seven empties on the other. The bow end had buffers fitted and so to load or unload the vessel had to turn and reverse into the dock. At Langston the end of the left-hand pier had a sloped timber jetty projecting down into the sea at an angle of 1 in 8 from the top of the quay to a point four feet below the sea bed. Railway lines were laid on the jetty to the same gauge as that on the deck of the ship. It will be noted that a vessel up against the ramp would still leave a gap between its stern and the ramp, to overcome this a mobile cradle fitted with steam winding gear and mounted on 24 wheels raised or lowered a flat section of decking, with rails laid on it. Wagons were pushed onto the cradle which was then lowered to the level of the deck and then man-handled up to the buffers at the bow of the vessel. Unloading was simply the reverse of this procedure, except that the wagons were pulled onto the cradle by means of a steam winch. A similar arrangement was installed at St Helens Quay on the Isle of Wight.

This new service commenced on 1st August, 1884 and ran three times weekly in each direction, weather permitting. However, after only one year of operating the service the IOWMT found it was running at a loss, ran into financial difficulties and decided to get out of the business. In December 1885 the *Carrier*, the quays at Langston and St Helens and all IOWMT interests were, leased to the LBSCR. The following year, the Brighton company purchased the whole operation for the sum of £40,000.

The LBSCR found that it too had difficulties covering its running costs and other ventures were tried in a vain attempt to make the *Carrier* pay its way. One of the least successful came in 1887 when the old vessel was used to convey passengers around the Royal Navy laid out in review order to celebrate the 50th anniversary of Queen Victoria's accession to the throne. All did not go as planned though, during one trip round the Spithead Review, the *Carrier* preceded the Royal Yacht belching out thick black smoke; we are informed that the Queen was not amused. The Lords of the Admiralty made sure from then on that private vessels were precluded from the Review area.

The cross-Solent ferry continued to stay in the red, partly due to the lack of traffic and also because of the many cancelled trips due to bad weather. *Carrier* having been built to cope only with river work it found the often choppy Solent hard to manage. By 1888 the railway company had had enough and the service was discontinued in March of that year. *Carrier* was laid up at Newhaven and eventually sold to a Swedish shipping company in May 1892.

The landing stage at St Helens Quay and the Bembridge line were taken over

PS *Carrier*, built in 1858 as a ferry on the River Tay in Scotland and purchased in 1884 for the Langston Wharf-St Helens (IoW) route. She could carry up to 14 fully loaded goods wagons at one time, but was probably never asked to carry that number on this poorly-used route.
Author's Collection

All that remains of the Langston Wharf almost a century after closure. These few rotten stumps mark the site of the remarkable ramp and cradle used to load and unload goods wagons from the PS *Carrier*.   *Author*

by the Isle of Wight Railway in 1898, but the Langston Harbour Wharf continued to be owned by the LBSCR until the end. Coasters still called in to Langston but by the early 1890s it had become so badly silted up that it was no longer viable.

In 1890 the goods depot was closed and before 1900 most of the sidings had been lifted. By 1920 only single sidings remained on either side of the Hayling Island branch line. As part of the Beeching rationalisation the entire branch line was closed on 2nd November, 1963.

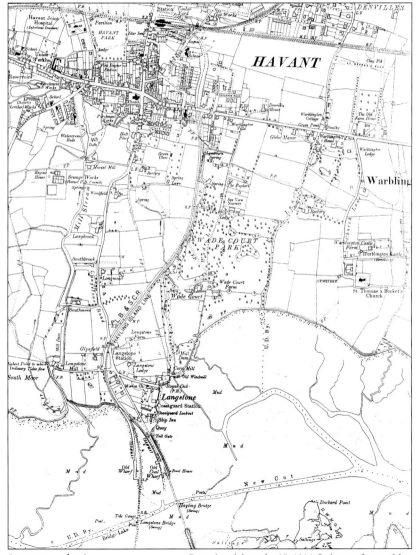

Langstone wharf.   *Reproduced from the 6", 1914 Ordnance Survey Map*

Deptford wharf.

Reproduced from the 25", 1916 Ordnance Survey Map

Appendix One

The London Wharves

Deptford Wharf

The London and Croydon Railway, as one of its last acts before amalgamating with the London and Brighton Railway to form the London, Brighton and South Coast Railway, placed before Parliament a Bill for a line to be built from New Cross to Deptford to be known as the Thames Junction Railway. Permission was granted under 9 & 10 Vict. cap. 63 dated 27th July, 1846, the same day as the Act was passed forming the LBSCR. The contract for the line was let to a Mr Rigby of Hollywell and signed in February 1847. Work was halted the following October when the LBSCR ran so short of money that bankruptcy loomed. With cash very tight only those new lines that had a guaranteed profit were allowed to proceed. At a shareholders' meeting in February 1848 it was decided that the cargo traffic from the new wharves at Deptford would merit the finishing of the line, and so work recommenced. An advertisement in *The Times* announced the completion of the line thus:

London, Brighton and South Coast Railway Thames Junction Branch

This line now open for goods traffic, the Waterside Business of the Company is Removed from Cold Blow Wharf, at New Cross, to the new station on the Thames at Deptford. Rates and particulars may be obtained on applying to G. Hawkins, Goods Manager, New Cross. July 2, 1849.

The line from New Cross station passed over the Grand Surrey Canal by means of a movable bridge, then under the Greenwich viaduct, climbed again over a road then re-crossed the Grand Survey Canal before dropping down to ground level. A fan of sidings crossed Grove Road before reaching the wharf. Locomotives were not allowed to cross the road, so wagons had to be towed by rope and capstan.

In 1851 authority was gained to build a branch off the Deptford Wharf line to the Surrey Commercial Docks, and this was opened in July 1855. To improve the flow of traffic through the wharf, wet docks were built in 1868 allowing the passage of barges at all states of the tide. Principal cargoes at this time were coal for the nearby railway coking plant, stone, minerals and timber. The following year the adjacent Deptford Dockyard was closed down and the Foreign Cattle Market built on the site. Although the LBSCR had access to the cattle market trade it was restricted by the confines of the wharf. It was decided in 1897, therefore, to apply for powers to build a branch from Deptford Wharf into the Foreign Cattle Market. These powers were granted under the Foreign Cattle Market, Deptford, Act 61 & 62 Vict. cap. 51 on 1st July, 1898. The line was opened in 1900 and was worked by horses towing the cattle trucks to the capstan at the wharf. Deptford Wharf outlasted the LBSCR by 42 years, finally being closed by British Railways in 1964.

Battersea wharf.

Reproduced from the 25", 1869 Ordnance Survey Map

Battersea wharf.

Reproduced from the 25", 1894 Ordnance Survey Map

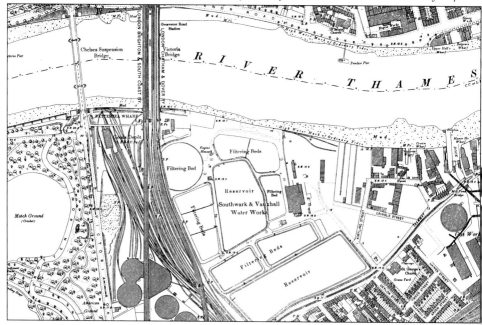

Battersea Wharf

In 1858 the LBSCR leased the West End Railway's Crystal Palace to Pimlico line. Pimlico station had sidings running down to wharves on the Thames at Battersea. Until Victoria station was opened in 1860 Pimlico was the London terminus of the LBSCR. On 1st October, 1860 Victoria opened and Pimlico was closed to passenger traffic, the whole being renamed Battersea Wharf.

The GNR, MR and LSWR also had running powers over this line and all made use of this Thames-side wharf for shipping livestock and goods into the capital.

In 1862 the wharf was improved with the building of further sidings, and by 1868 wet docks had been built at the wharf. Although barges carried most of the goods into the London wharves, LBSCR's own vessels occasionally steamed up the Thames from Newhaven to both Battersea and Deptford Wharves. Battersea Wharf was closed by British Railways in 1964.

Wagon label from Battersea Wharf, 1902.   *Author's Collection*

House Flags of the LBSCR

LBSCR Newhaven-Dieppe 1860s-1887
Blue flag with a white St Andrew's cross.

LBSCR Newhaven-Caen 1887-1923
White flag with a blue St Andrew's cross, with a small red St Andrew's cross in the centre

LBSCR-Ouest Newhaven-Dieppe 1887-1923
White flag with red St George's cross, corners alternately red and blue.

Royal Mail Pennant
White pennant with 'ROYAL MAIL' in red bisected by a post horn surmounted by a crown.

Key

☐ White   ■ Blue   ▨ Red

Appendix Three
Vessel Technical Data

Newhaven-Dieppe

Name	Built Acquired Disposed	Builder	Length ft	Width ft	Depth ft	Gross Tonnage	No. of Cyl.	Cyl. size in.	Stroke in.	HP	Remarks
Brighton (I)	1847 1847 1850	Thompson, Rotherhithe	153.6	21.2	11.9	263.4				80	Brighton & Continental Steam Packet Co.
Dieppe (I)	1847 1847 1857	Thompson, Rotherhithe	153.6	21.2	11.9	263.4				80	Brighton & Continental Steam Packet Co.
Newhaven (I)	1847 1847 1852	Thompson, Rotherhithe	153.6	21.2	11.9	263.4				80	Brighton & Continental Steam Packet Co.
Ayreshire Lassie	1839 - 1852	R. Duncan & Co., Greenock	123.8	18.1	8.7	169					Maples
Culloden	1845 - 1852	Denny, Dumbarton	145	16.5	8.6	250	1			100	Maples
Rothesay Castle	1837 - 1851	Tod & McGregor	133.8	17	8.6	180	1	52½	48	92	Maples
Ladybird	1851 1854	Denny, Dumbarton	160			176	2	36, 27		150	Charter
Samuel Laing	1854 - 1859	Palmer, Newcastle	164.8	26.6	15.8	606				40	Charter Owner-Taylor & Co.

Name	Built Acquired Disposed	Builder	Length ft	Width ft	Depth ft	Gross Tonnage	No. of Cyl.	Cyl. size in.	Stroke in.	HP	Remarks
William Cory	1857 - -	Newcastle									Charter
Jas Dixon	- 1854 -									120	Charter
Cockerill	- 1854 -							12"			Charter
Vigilant	- 1854 -	Hull								50	Charter
Staffa	- 1867 -										Charter
Duntroon Castle	1842 1857 1863	Anderson & Gilmour	140.1	21	10.2	258	1			150	Maples
Dieppe (2)	1853 1855 1859-1867	London	181.5	19.8	10.7	360				150	Maples
London	1853 1853 1850s	Glasgow	194	21	12	341				126	Maples
Paris	1852 1852 1863	Port Glasgow	165	20.1	9.2	350				120	Maples
Collier	1848 1854 1857	John Reid & Co., Port Glasgow	95	20		116				40	Maples
Brighton (2)	1856 1857 185?	Palmers Ship & Iron Co., Jarrow	193.5	20.9	10	286	2	44, 48	48	128	

Menai	– – –										GSNC
Fame	– – –										GSNC
Magician	1842 –		146			175					GSNC
Wave Queen	1852 – –	J. Scott Russel, London	200	13		196				80	Maples
Aquilla	– – –	J. Henderson, Renfrew	180.4	21		264	2	42, 42		110	Charter
Trident	– – –										Hopper vessel
Marco	1854 – –	Jersey				58					
Rouen (I)	1853 – 1859-1862	J. Scott Russel, London	180	20	9.5	357				120	Ex-Maples
Orleans	1856 – 1878	J. Scott Russel, London	187.2	21.6	9.7	270	2	48, 48	54	160	Ex-Maples
Lyons	1856 – 1885	J. Scott Russel, London	189.2	21.8	9.7	269	2	48, 48	54	160	Ex-Maples
Alar	1847 1857 –	Neath	138	17.8	9.1	150				50	
Alexandra	1863 1863 1883	Caird, Glasgow	204.5	23.7	11	332	2	52, 52	57	200	Ex-Maples

Name	Built Acquired Disposed	Builder	Length ft	Width ft	Depth ft	Gross Tonnage	No. of Cyl.	Cyl. size in.	Stroke in.	HP	Remarks
Normandy (Rouen from 1882)	1863 1863 1889	Richardson & Co., Newcastle	112.6	17.9	10.2	149	1	22	20	40	Ex-Maples
Sussex	1862 1862 1887	Richardson & Co., Newcastle	110	17.8	9.9	178	2	22, 22	20	32	Ex-Maples
Rouen (2)	1863 1863 1889	Richardson & Co., Newcastle	112.6	17.9	9.9	180	2	22, 22	20	32	Ex-Maples
Marseilles	1864 1864 1892	C. Lungley, Deptford	213.9	23.4	11.3	432	2	52, 52	57	180	Ex-Maples
Bordeaux	1865 1865 1890	Charles Lungley, Deptford, London	214	23.7	10.8	432	2	52, 52	57	200	Ex-Maples
Dieppe	1875 1875 1901	Forges et Chantiers de la Mediteranee, Havre	168.4	21.1	11.9	432	4	2x24½, 2x39½	23¾	120	
Newhaven	1875 1875 1899	Forges et Chantiers de la Mediteranee, Havre	168.4	21.1	11.9	326	2	24¾, 39½	24	120	
Paris (I)	1875 1875 1888	John Elder & Co., Glasgow	220	25.2	11	483	2	41, 72	60	220	
Brighton (2)	1878 1878 1893	John Elder & Co., Glasgow	221.3	27.7	10.6	531	2	48, 83	60	300	
Victoria	1878 1878 1887	John Elder & Co., Glasgow	221.3	27.7	10.6	533	2	48, 83	60	300	
Normandy (I)	1882 1882 188?	John Elder & Co., Glasgow	231	27.7	10.6	529	2	46, 83¾	60	60	

Ship				Builder	Length	Beam	Depth	Tonnage	No.	Cylinders	Stroke	Power	Notes
Brittany (I)	1882	1882	1901	John Elder & Co., Glasgow	231	27.7	10.6	579	2	46, 83	60	350	
Italy (Italie from 1887)	1885	1885	1910	John Elder & Co., Glasgow	190.6	26.1	14	487	6	2x22, 4x32	24	250	
Lyons (2) (Lyon from 1887)	1885	1885	1911	John Elder & Co., Glasgow	190.6	26.1	14	487	6	2x22, 4x32	24	250	
Paris (2)	1888	1888	1912	Fairfield & Co., Glasgow	250.6	29.1	14	761	2	46, 83	72	450	
Rouen (3)	1888	1888	1903	Fairfield & Co., Glasgow	250.6	29.1	14	804	2	46, 83	72	450	
Angers	1890	1890	1899	Societes des Forges et Chantiers de la Mediteranee, Havre	210.6	26.3	13.6	522	6	16½, 24½, 37 2 each	25½	115	Sunk
Caen	1890	1890	1913	Societes des Forges et Chantiers de la Mediteranee, Havre	210.6	26.3	13.6	522	6	16½, 24½, 37 2 each	25½	115	
Seine	1891	1891	1906	Societes des Forges et Chantiers de la Mediteranee, Havre	268.9	29.7	15.6	808	6	24, 36, 55 2 each	25½	4,000 rpm	Turbine
Tamise	1893	1893	1913	Societes des Forges et Chantiers de la Mediteranee, Havre	269	29.5	15.1	978	3	23½, 35½, 51½ 2 each	25½	4,500 rpm	Turbine
Seaford	1894	1894	1895	W. Denny & Bros, Dumbarton	262.8	34	13.9	900	8	Triple-twin expansion 2x23½, 2x32½, 4x37½	27	5,000 rpm	Turbine, sunk
Trouville (I)	1894	1894	1901	Wm Denny & Bros, Dumbarton	195	28.1	14.3	570	6	13½, 20½, 31 2 each	21	104	
Calvados (I)	1894	1894	1901	Wm Denny & Bros, Dumbarton	195	28.1	14.3	570	6	13½, 20½, 31 2 each	21	104	

SS *Arundel* leaving Newhaven harbour.

Name	Built / Acquired / Disposed	Builder	Length ft	Width ft	Depth ft	Gross Tonnage	No. of Cyl.	Cyl. size in.	Stroke in.	HP	Remarks
Sussex	1896 1896 1916	Wm Denny & Bros, Dumbarton	275	34.1	14.3	1,117	8	2x23½, 2x35, 4x37	27	5,000	Turbine, war loss
Prince Arthur	1896 1896 1901	Wm Denny & Bros, Dumbarton	195	28.1	14.3	581	6	13½, 20½, 31 2 each	21	104	
Manche	1896 1897 1913	Forges et Chantiers de la Mediteranee, Havre	269	29.5	15.1	978	6	23½, 35½, 51½ 2 each	25½	5,000 rpm	Turbine.
La France	1899 1899 1922	Forges et Chantiers de la Mediteranee, Havre	264	29.5	15.1	1,059	6	24¾, 35⁵⁄₁₆, 53⅜ 2 each	25⁵⁄₁₆	5,000 rpm	Turbine.
Brest	1900 1900 1939-45	Soiciete des Forges et Chantiers de la Mediteranee, Havre	204	26	15	530	6	11, 17½, 25½ 2 each	18	560	
Cherbourg	1900 1900 1917	Soiciete des Forges et Chantiers de la Mediteranee, Havre	204	26	15	530	6	11, 17½, 25½ 2 each	18	560	
Arundel	1900 1900 1934	Denny, Dumbarton	269.1	34.1	14.1	1,067	8	2x23½, 2x35¼, 4x37½	27	5,000	
Cavados Ex-Paris	1878 1901 1911	Scott of Greenock	170.7	22.7	12.5	330	2	25½, 46½	24	85	
Trouville Ex-Roubaix	1874 1901 1911	J.W. Dudgeon, London	161.2	22.2	12.2	316	2	24¾, 45	24	80	
Portsmouth	1902 1902 1935	Soiciete des Forges et Chantiers de la Mediteranee, Havre	204	26	15	530	6	11, 17½, 25½ 2 each	18	560	
Brighton (4)	1903 1903 1930	Denny, Dumbarton	273.6	34.2	14.1	1,129	T	Parsons triple turbine	-	6,000 rpm	Triple screw.

The TrSS *Brighton*.

Name	Built Acquired Disposed	Builder	Length ft	Width ft	Depth ft	Gross Tonnage	No. of Cyl.	Cyl. size in.	Stroke in.	HP	Remarks
Dieppe (2)	1905 1905 1933	Fairfield, Glasgow	274	34.8	13.9	1,215	T	Steam turbine	-	6,500 rpm	Triple screw.
Normandy (2)	1910 1910 1912	Earles & Co., Hull	192	29	14	614	3	$15\frac{1}{2}$, 25, 40	27	614	Newhaven-Caen via Oustreham canal route
Brittany (2)	1910 1910 1912	Earles & Co., Hull	192	22.9	14.1	618	3	$13\frac{1}{2}$, 25, 40	27	82	
Maine	1910 1910 1917	Ateliers et Chantiers de la Loire, Nantes	209.2	27.9	16	773	6	14, 23, 38 2 each	30	1,525 rpm	War loss.
Anjou	1910 1910 1918	Ateliers et Chantiers de la Loire, Nantes	209.2	27.9	15	771	6	$13\frac{1}{2}$, 23, 38 2 each	30	6,500 rpm	War loss.
Newhaven (2)	1911 1911 1945	Forges et Chantiers de la Mediteranee, Havre	292	34.6	22.1	1,656	T	Triple steam turbine	-	10,000 rpm	Turbine.
Rouen (4)	1911 1911 1940	Forges et Chantiers de la Mediteranee, Havre	292	34.6	22.1	1,656	T	Triple steam turbine	-	10,000 rpm	Turbine.
Bordeaux (2)	1912 1912 1951	Ateliers et Chantiers de la Loire, Nantes	206.7	27.9	15.9	774	6	14, $22\frac{27}{32}$, $37\frac{13}{16}$ 2 each	$29\frac{15}{16}$	1400	Turbine.
Paris (3)	1913 1913 1940	Denny, Dumbarton	293.5	35.5	15.2	1,774	T	Geared comp. single reduction turbines	-	14,000	Turbine.
Versailles	1919 1921 1944	Forges et Chantiers de la Meditierenee, Havre	300.6	34.6	21.4	1,903	T	Twin steam turbine		15,000	Turbine.

808 — DIEPPE.
Le Paquebot "Versailles", dans les Jetées.
The Mail-Steamer "Versailles" into the Piers.

TrSS *Versailles* approaches Dieppe.

Newhaven Harbour Company

Name	Built	Acquired	Disposed	Builder	Length ft	Width ft	Depth ft	Gross Tonnage	No. of Cyl.	Cyl. size in.	Stroke in.	HP	Remarks
SR9		1902	-	Newhaven				42					Coal lighter
SR10		1910	-	Southampton				46					Coal lighter
SR10	-	1902	-	Newhaven				42					Coal lighter
SR11	-	1910	-	J. Dibble & Sons									Coal lighter
SR12	-	1907	-	Littlehampton									Coal lighter
SR13	-	1907	-	Littlehampton				45					Coal lighter
SR14	-	1913	-	Portsmouth									Coal lighter
Albert	1898	1901	1926-32	Woolston	116	20.1	9.8	175				66	
Foremost 22	1924	1925		J. Myers & Co., Zaltbommel	100.4	27.2	12.2	211	3	15, 25, 40	27	110	Ordered by LBSCR
Hauler	-	1905	-	New Holland	55	14.1	5.9	31				35	Tug

Name	Built / Acquired / Disposed	Builder	Length ft	Width ft	Depth ft	Gross Tonnage	No. of Cyl.	Cyl. size in.	Stroke in.	HP	Remarks
Imp	1900 / 1919 / –	New Holland	26.3	6.1	1.7	3					Launch
Leven	1885 / 1894 / 1905	Renfrew	185.3	38.6	14.9	775				120	Dredger
Neptune	– / 1877 / –	W. Simmons & Co.									Dredger
Nitrogen	1912 / 1928	Hepple & Co., South Shields	79	17.1	6.7	78	2	13, 13	13⅜	23	Oil barge
North Kent	1863 / 1881-84 / 1884-1886	Rochester	94.5	12.6	6.5	46				24	Tug
Pinafore	– / 1880 / 1902	Brighton	36	11.7	5.2	27				15	Tender / fire tug
Richmere	1915 / 1921-23 / 1949	G. Brown & Co., Greenock	59.3	14.7	6.7	48				5	Tug
Soton	1915 / 1919	Sunderland Shipbuilding Co.	104	22		145				102	Lighter
Sultan	– / 1895 / 1919										Launch

Langston-IOW Route

Name	Built / Acquired / Disposed	Builder	Length ft	Width ft	Depth ft	Gross Tonnage	No. of Cyl.	Cyl. size in.	Stroke in.	HP	Remarks
Carrier	1858 / 1884 / 1889	Scotts Shipbuilding & Engineering Co.,	124	24.7	8.5	243	2	42, 42	36	112	Ex-IOW Marine Transit Co. Ltd

Portsmouth-Ryde (IOW)

Prince Consort	1859 1859 1882	J. Scot Russel, London	154.5	15.1	6.7	104	2	30, 30	30	60	Ex-PP&RUSPCo.
Princess of Wales	1865 1865 1885	Lewis & Stockwell, London	152.4	16.0	6.9	150	2	32, 32	30	50	Ex-PP&RUSPCo.
Duke of Edinburgh	1869 1869 c. 1884	Money, Wigram Co., Blackwall	136.2	14.1	7.0	95	2			50	Ex-PP&RUSPCo.
Princess Alice	1869 1869 1882	Money, Wigram Co., Blackwall	136.2	14.1	7.0	95	2			50	Ex-PP&RUSPCo.
Heather Bell	1871 1876 1899	Blackwood & Gordon, Glasgow	207.7	21.0	8.8	268	2	40, 60	66	150	Ex-PP&RUSPCo. Sold to South Coast Continental Service Co.
Albert Edward	1878 1878 1893	Oswald Mordaunt, Southampton	169.4	20.5	9.0	269	2	26, 50	51	120	Ex-PP&RUSPCo. Sold to Mr David MacBrayne
Alexandra	1879 1879 1913	Scott & Co., Greenock	171.0	20.2	8.5	235	2	25, 50	54	170	Ex-PP&RUSPCo. Sold to Bembridge and Seaview Steam Packet Co.
Victoria	1881 1881 1899	Aitken & Mansel, Glasgow	191.9	25.1	8.6	366	2	32, 57	54	160	Sold to Southampton, IOW & South of England Royal Mail Steam Packet Co.
Duchess of Connaught	1884 1884 1910	Aitken & Mansel, Glasgow	190.6	26.1	8.8	342	2	32, 55	60	195	Sold overseas
Duchess of Edinburgh	1884 1884 1910	Aitken & Mansel, Glasgow	190.6	26.1	8.8	342	2	32, 55	60	195	Sold overseas
Duchess of Albany	1889 1889 1928	Scott & Co., Greenock	170.4	22.1	8.5	256	2	23, 54	54	256	Replaced by PS *Merstone*.

Name	Built Acquired Disposed	Builder	Length ft	Width ft	Depth ft	Gross Tonnage	No. of Cyl.	Cyl. size in.	Stroke in.	HP	Remarks
Princess Margaret	1893 1893 1928	Scott & Co., Greenock	170.6	22.1	8.5	260	2	23, 54	54	150	Replaced by PS Portsdown
Duchess of Kent	1897 1897 1933	Day, Summers & Co., Southampton	195.4	26.1	9.0	399	2	32, 59	60	225	Replaced by PS Sandown Sold to New Medway Steam Packet Co.
Duchess of Fife	1899 1899 1929	Clydebank Engineering & Shipbuilding Co., Glasgow	215.0	26.6	9.2	400	2	26, 55	54	185	Broken up
Duchess of Richmond	1910 1910 1915	D. & W. Henderson, Glasgow	190.2	26.1	8.7	354	2	27, 51	54	206	Mined while on war service.
Duchess of Norfolk	1911 1911 1937	D. & W. Henderson, Glasgow	190.0	26.1	8.7	281	2	27, 51	54	159	Sold to Cosens & Co. Ltd, Weymouth
Horseboat 1	1870 1870 1920s	Read	45.5	16.2	2.0	19					Tow boat
Horseboat 2	1870 - -	Hayle									Tow boat
Horseboat 3	1864 1912										Tow boat
Horseboat 4	1904 - -										Tow boat
Horseboat 5	1912 - -										Tow boat

Name	Dates	Builder	Length	Beam	Depth	Tonnage					Notes
Enterprise	1879 1879 1900										Coal hulk
Dragon	1880		180.0	36.0	16.5						Coal hulk
Un-named	- 1902 -	Armstrong Whitworth, London	164.0	33.3		700					Coal hulk, Portsmouth
Ada	1903 1903 1910										Launch
Ada	1910 1910 1917										Launch
Aid	- - 1916										Launch
Adur II	1912 1919 1925	Heppie & Co., South Shields	70.3	15.9	7.2	54		13, 26	18	40	Tug boat

Littlehampton-France

Name	Dates	Builder	Length	Beam	Depth	Tonnage				
Ida	1858 1863 1890	Stockton	137.7	20.2		221		25, 25	24	50
Rennes	1865 1866 1891	Millwall Iron Works, London	159.9	23	10.8	289	8	4x13, 4x27	20	100
Viking	1871 1872 1895	Swan & Co., Dumbarton	120.5	19.8	9.8	194	2	16, 26	22	40
Honfleur	1875 1875 1897	Gourley Bros, Dundee	150.4	20.9	11.7	306	2	18, 34	18	50

References

Publications

A Century Of Cross Channel Passenger Ferries by A. Greenway
Famous Paddle Steamers by F.C. Hambleton
Lloyds Register Of Shipping. Various 1830-1920
London, Brighton And South Coast Railway by C. Hamilton Ellis (Ian Allan)
London, Brighton And South Coast Railway by J.T. Howard Turner (Batsford)
London And Its Railways by R. Davies & M.D. Grant
LBSCR 'Formation Of Main Line And Suburban Trains' July 1908
LBSCR Timetable October 1922
LBSCR Works Specifications, Various 1873-1910
LBSCR-French State Railways Continental Timetable Winter 1911-1912
LBSCR-Western Railway Of France Steam Packet Service Timetable November/December 1886
Newhaven-Dieppe by B.M.E. O'Mahony
Railway and Other Steamers by Duckworth & Langmuir (Stephenson)
Various Acts Of Parliament

Maps

OS	60/NW	6 in.	1914	Hayling Island
OS	63/13	25 in.	1876	Littlehampton
OS	78/7	25 in.	1872	Newhaven
OS	78/3	25 in.	1872	Newhaven
OS	78/7-11	25 in.	1899	Newhaven
OS	78/3	25 in.	1899	Newhaven
OS	78/7-11	25 in.	1910	Newhaven
OS		25 in.	1896	Portsmouth

Littlehampton Branch Railway 1845 & 1858/59
LBSCR Various Powers 1866

The *Duchess of Norfolk* was the final vessel built for the LBSC/LSWR joint fleet. It was purchased by Cosens & Co. of Weymouth from the Southern Railway in 1937 and was renamed the *Embassy*. It is seen here being towed away from Weymouth harbour on 25th May, 1967 by tug *Fairplay II* on her last journey to Dutch breakers. The final LBSC vessel leaving British waters for the last time. *C.L. Caddy Collection*